T0279821

A ROTTEN CROWD

A Rotten Crowd

America, Wealth, and One Hundred Years
of *The Great Gatsby*

John Marsh

MONTHLY REVIEW PRESS

New York

Copyright © 2024 by John Marsh
All Rights Reserved

Library of Congress Cataloging-in-Publication Data
available from the publisher.

ISBN: 978-168590-083-0 cloth

Typeset in Bulmer MT

Monthly Review Press | New York
www.monthlyreview.org

5 4 3 2 1

CONTENTS

Acknowledgments

A writer accrues a lot of debts. I would like to thank everyone at Monthly Review Press: Martin Paddio, Rebecca Manski, Erin Clermont, and especially Michael Yates, who has saved me from more than one harebrained argument. Thank you to James L. W. West III, who knows more about Fitzgerald than I—or anyone—ever will and who read a late draft of this book. Thanks to Richard Doyle, who was a friend when I needed one, and to Jennifer Thomson, we're off the streets now. Finally, to Nora Marsh, who, as Nick says to Gatsby, is worth the whole damn bunch put together.

The Great Gatsby in 1,000 Words

I hope this book inspires its readers to read (or more likely re-read) *The Great Gatsby*. But if you have never read the novel, or have not read it for a while, here is a cast of characters (in order of appearance) and a summary.

NICK CARRAWAY, narrator of the book and
    Gatsby's friend
DAISY BUCHANAN, Nick's cousin
TOM BUCHANAN, Daisy's wealthy husband
JORDAN BAKER, Daisy's girlhood friend
JAY GATSBY (né James Gatz), bootlegger who
    comes east to win Daisy back
MYRTLE WILSON, Tom's mistress
GEORGE WILSON, Myrtle's husband
MEYER WOLFSHEIM, racketeer

A Rotten Crowd

When the novel opens, it is 1922, and Nick Carraway is back in his hometown of St. Paul, Minnesota, writing a book about the events of the previous summer.

A veteran of the First World War, Nick leaves St. Paul to learn the bond business in New York City. He rents a ramshackle house on Long Island abutting a garish mansion that, he later learns, belongs to one Jay Gatsby. Nick has dinner with a distant cousin, Daisy Buchanan, and her obscenely wealthy husband, Tom Buchanan, whom Nick knows from their time at Yale. Also at dinner is Jordan Baker, a childhood friend of Daisy's and a professional golfer whom Nick will eventually date. The dinner grows awkward when Tom launches into a diatribe about "the colored races" and is called away to the phone, twice, to speak to his mistress. After dinner, Nick returns home and watches from afar as a man, Gatsby, stands on the lawn of his mansion holding his arms out toward a green light across the bay, where Daisy lives.

In the second chapter, Tom takes Nick to New York on the commuter train, which passes through a grotesque "valley of ashes": mountains upon mountains of spent coal and garbage. On a tired street running alongside it, an equally tired man, George Wilson, runs a gas station and car repair shop. His wife, Myrtle Wilson, is having an affair with Tom. Tom drags Nick off the train so he can meet Myrtle. He tells her to take the next train to New York. There, Tom, Nick, Myrtle, and some of her friends have a boozy party in the apartment Tom rents for Myrtle. The party ends with Tom breaking

Myrtle's nose for repeating the name of his wife, which Tom has forbidden.

The third chapter is devoted to one of the decadent parties Gatsby regularly throws at his mansion. Nick finds Jordan at the party, where he meets the mysterious Gatsby for the first time. At the end of the party, Gatsby takes Jordan aside to tell her why he has moved to Long Island. Before the war, he had been stationed in Louisville, Kentucky, where he met and fell in love with Daisy and she with him. After the war, Gatsby, stranded in Europe and dirt poor anyway, cannot marry Daisy, so she marries Tom Buchanan instead.

Soon after his talk with Jordan, Gatsby drives Nick to New York where they meet Meyer Wolfsheim for lunch. Wolfsheim, a gambler and racketeer, has made Gatsby rich by setting him up as a bootlegger and handler of fraudulent bonds. Later, over tea, Jordan will tell Nick what Gatsby told her at the party, which is that Gatsby has bought his mansion to be close to Daisy so he can make her fall in love with him again. Jordan tells Nick that Gatsby wants him to invite Daisy to his house so that he, Gatsby, can "accidentally" happen upon her. Nick does, and Gatsby and Daisy reunite and renew their love for each other. Gatsby takes Nick and Daisy on a tour of his mansion, hoping to impress her and show that he has overcome the poverty that earlier kept them apart. Gatsby and Daisy begin an affair.

The novel reaches its climax when Gatsby, Tom, Daisy, Nick, and Jordan escape the heat by driving into Manhattan and taking a room at the Plaza Hotel. Tom drives a yellow car that belongs to Gatsby, and Gatsby and Daisy ride in a car that belongs to Tom. This detail will matter. On the way to New York, Tom learns that George has discovered that Myrtle is having an affair and has locked her in an upstairs bedroom. At the hotel, Gatsby announces his love for Daisy, and Daisy tells Tom that she is leaving him. Tom bullies Daisy into staying with him by revealing the sordid ways Gatsby has made his money and to whom and what she would be attaching herself if she married him. On the drive home, Myrtle, thinking that the yellow car Daisy is driving belongs to Tom, rushes into the road and is run over—and killed—by Daisy. The accident leads Daisy to reunite with Tom.

George Wilson, unhinged by the death of his wife, sets out to find who killed her. He first goes to Tom, who tells him that the car that killed his wife belongs to Gatsby, which is true enough. What he does not say, either because Daisy has not told him or he is covering for her, is that Daisy was driving the car. Wilson tracks down Gatsby and kills him and then himself. The final chapter of the novel describes how Nick arranges a funeral for Gatsby and tries, with little success, to get people to come. Tom and Daisy have absconded, and not even Wolfsheim, with whom Gatsby was closest, attends.

The novel ends with Nick disgusted at what has happened, especially with Tom and Daisy and the whole "rotten crowd" of the rich who can smash "up things and creatures," retreat into their money, and leave others to clean up the mess.

Nick returns to St. Paul. His closing thoughts turn to what the Dutch sailors who "discovered" America must have thought when they first encountered the continent. They are likened to Gatsby, who had a similar wonder for Daisy. The novel closes with some of the most famous sentences in American literature:

> Gatsby believed in the green light, the orgastic future that year by year recedes before us. It eluded us then, but that's no matter—tomorrow we will run faster, stretch out our arms further. . . . And one fine morning—
>
> So we beat on, boats against the current, borne back ceaselessly into the past.

The Distressing Proximity of Millionaires

That was always my experience—a poor boy in a rich town; a poor boy in a rich boy's school; a poor boy in a rich man's club at Princeton. . . . However, I have never been able to forgive the rich for being rich, and it has colored my entire life and works.

—F. SCOTT FITZGERALD

A whole book about another book? Yes, and here's why.

This year marks the 100th anniversary of F. Scott Fitzgerald's *The Great Gatsby*. That by itself would merit a return to the novel. Beginning in the early 1960s, *The Great Gatsby* wormed its way into high school and college class-rooms and, even after wave after wave of educational reform, remains there today. As late as 2008, half of all high school students in the country had read it.[1] As of 2013, the novel still sold 500,000 copies per year.[2] If Americans share a common book—besides the Bible—it is *The Great Gatsby*. It is not canonical but, as one scholar put it, hyper-canonical.[3]

More than just round numbers, however, turn our attention back to *The Great Gatsby*. Consider the graph on the next page. It depicts how much wealth in the United States belonged and belongs to the top .01 percent of households. Not the infamous top 1 percent but rather the top .01 percent, the richest of the rich. The peak on the left represents the share of wealth (around 10 percent) owned by the top .01 percent in 1929. The peak on the right represents the share of wealth (again around 10 percent) owned by the top .01 percent in 2018.[4] There is every reason to believe that this latter share has risen since 2018. I call them the "Gatsby Peaks."[5] Notice as well that the tax burden of these ultra-wealthy households has fallen considerably.

The United States of 1925, when *The Great Gatsby* appeared, differed radically from the United States of today. Then, radio was the revolutionary communication technology. Today, of course, it is social media. Then, approximately one-third of Americans lived on farms. Today, about one out of every hundred does. Then, there was roughly one car on the road for every five people. Today, there are nearly as many cars as there are people.

Americans of 1925 and 2025 do have one thing in common, though, which is that they lived in a world where an infinitesimal slice of the population claimed more wealth than

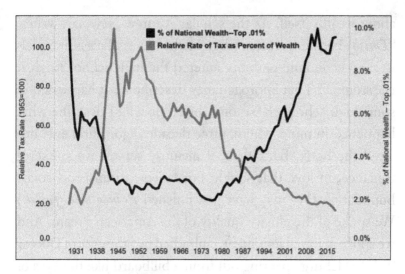

Figure 0.1: Share of Wealth and Tax Rate in the U.S. Owned by the Top .01 Percent of Households, 1931–2016 Source: https://taxprof. typepad.com/taxprof_blog/2021/02/the-unique-and-dominant-role-of-tax-policy-in-wealth-concentration.html

it had in generations. Among other reasons, this inequality is why *The Great Gatsby* matters. It was published during a period when every year the rich grew richer still. We live in a similar period. The novel offers archetypes of the wealthy that, like characters from the Brothers Grimm, still circulate today: Tom, the philandering, amoral brute; Daisy Buchanan, the beautiful, cosseted wife; and Jay Gatsby, the romantic, ostentatious arriviste.

For some literary critics, however, *The Great Gatsby* did not just depict the wealthy. It invited readers to think critically about wealth itself. As the scholar Andrew Newman writes, "*Gatsby* became a vector whereby the issues of class, inequality, and economic mobility entered the high school English classroom."[6] That approach may describe what happened in some high school classrooms, but it does not describe what happened in mine, where, three decades ago, I first encountered the book. Back then, if memory serves, we spoke of romance, of love that sought but failed to transcend social boundaries. (We may have just finished *Romeo and Juliet*.) We spoke of the elusive quality of the American dream. And we spoke of moral judgment, embodied by "the eyes of Doctor T. J. Eckleburg" peering out from a billboard like the eyes of God. Nowhere, however, did we speak of class, inequality, or economic mobility. As a poor boy in a middle-class town, I would have been all ears if we had.

I cannot know what happened in every high school English classroom of the last half century, but I suspect my experience with the text is more representative than not. In this book, I discuss what you should have discussed when you read *The Great Gatsby*. Not just class, inequality, and economic mobility—though I examine those at length—but also immigration, racism, anti-Semitism, and, of a piece with these, the power, privilege, and impunity that wealth can buy for those who have it.

The Great Gatsby is not, however, a pure indictment of the rich. It would not work as well as a novel if it were. Rather, *The Great Gatsby* takes advantage of popular fascination with the rich—their houses, their clothes, their manners—only to reveal how misguided (Gatsby) or inhuman (Tom, Daisy, Jordan) its rich truly are. Only someone like Fitzgerald, who simultaneously envied and resented the rich, could write such a book. That is what makes him—and his narrator, Nick Carraway—such a perceptive guide to this world.[7] Like Nick, Fitzgerald "was within and without, simultaneously enchanted and repelled by the inexhaustible variety of life," including the lives of the rich.[8] In trying to keep up with the wealthy, Fitzgerald spent the better part of his adult life in debt. Yet he often recognized not just the futility of trying to keep up with the rich but the emptiness of doing so.

Perhaps because its narrator—and its author—stands "within and without," *The Great Gatsby* tells readers less about wealth, though it certainly does that, than it does about how it feels to live among the wealthy, to live in a world shaped by the extreme concentration of wealth. Although it may seem that the wealthy live at some distant remove, in reality what they do and say trickles down and pools at our feet.

In the chapters that follow, I explore what Fitzgerald has to say in *The Great Gatsby* about wealth, the wealthy, and life among wealth and the wealthy. I follow him in focusing on four themes: clothes, waste, bonds, and race. Each chapter eventually expands to consider what those concepts mean today. How do the clothes people wear signal their wealth— or their aspirations to wealth? What kinds of waste—economic, environmental, emotional—accompany a culture of wealth? What kinds of relationships do the wealthy—*must* the wealthy—form with others? Finally, how does racism constrain the options a nation has for reining in runaway wealth? In a conclusion, I suggest what we could do about the concentration of wealth today to lessen the damage it does to ourselves and our culture.

I

Near the end of the novel, after Daisy accidentally kills Myrtle and conspires to avoid the consequences, Gatsby and Nick return home to Gatsby's mansion. As Nick leaves, he pays Gatsby "the only compliment" he ever gave him: "'They're a rotten crowd,' he shouts to Gatsby from across the lawn. "'You're worth the whole damn bunch put together.'" Here, Tom, Daisy, and Jordan form a "they." But that "they" includes more than just Tom, Daisy, and Jordan. If Andrew Newman is right that "*Gatsby* became a vector whereby the issues of class, inequality, and economic mobility entered the high school English classroom," then the "they" in the "rotten crowd" encompasses not just Tom and Daisy but the rich more generally.[9]

Yet the extrapolation from Tom and Daisy to all the wealthy everywhere poses a problem, namely stereotyping. Unlike Tom, not every rich man, then or now, has affairs with working-class women or breaks their noses for mouthing off. Unlike Daisy, not every rich woman conspires to escape the consequences of what is at best a horrible accident and at worst manslaughter. And unlike Jordan, not every rich woman

18

cheats at golf or pouts when her boyfriend does not feel like keeping the party going despite having recently witnessed a gruesome death. ("It's only half-past nine," Jordan tells Nick.) Yet generations of readers have taken Tom, Daisy, and Jordan not simply as themselves but as representative of the wealthy qua wealthy. Of course, that is how literature often works. Writers no longer turn out allegory, in which Everyman falls into a Slough of Despond as in *Pilgrim's Progress*. Still, we do tend to label anyone who falls from absolute power to complete feebleness as a King Lear.

But we would never, Rainer Zitelmann argues in *The Rich in Public Opinion*, accept stereotypes of other groups as we do stereotypes of the rich, many of which appear in and are affirmed by *The Great Gatsby*. Zitelmann attributes this hostility toward the rich to envy, which he defines as "an emotion that arises from the desire to acquire the other group's resources"[10] Nor is this envy benign. It births schadenfreude and, taken far enough, violence. "The 20th Century," Zitelmann writes, "is full of examples of rich people, including capitalists, kulaks, and other groups, who were victims of persecution."[11]

It would be tempting to dismiss Zitelmann as a crank or an apologist for the wealthy. For many people, stereotypes only become menacing when those who entertain them have the power to shape the lives of those with considerably less power. (Zitelmann raises this objection but never quite answers it.) Moreover, as he does with hostility toward the rich, Zitelmann ascribes any desire for egalitarianism to jealousy and quotes approvingly a line from the Spanish essayist Fernandez de la Mora that "equality is a paradisiacal promise for the envious, the definitive incentive."[12] In other words, if you want a world where wealth is more evenly distributed, you are an envious fantasist trying to assuage your own feelings of inferiority. Tempting indeed.

Yet grant Zitelmann this. Wealth in and of itself is not immoral.[13] Nor are the wealthy in and of themselves immoral. The wealthy may use their economic power to exercise more than their share of political power, but I doubt that few people, if they found themselves suddenly wealthy, would do otherwise.[14] No one likes to pay taxes, for example, and many people—including me—think they could put their tax money to better uses than whatever state or federal program they find unconscionable. (For my part, I do not understand why the United States has to devote as much money to defense spending as the next ten countries combined.)[15] In other words, we would do well to remember—and Zitelmann helps us remember—that neither virtue nor vice resides with one class alone.

Fitzgerald himself struggled to make these finer distinctions. "I have never been able to forgive the rich for being rich," he wrote to Anne Ober in 1938, and his language ("forgive") implies that the rich have sinned in becoming or being rich.[16] Most of them, of course, have not. As Gatsby says of Wolfsheim, they have merely taken advantage of an opportunity. That is why in the rest of this book I try, though

I may not always succeed, to speak of wealth or a culture of wealth instead of the wealthy. Regardless, the distribution of wealth matters, and we should not hesitate to say how and why. There is a substantial difference between living in a country where the top .01 percent of households own between 2 and 3 percent of the wealth of a nation, as they did in the decades after the Second World War, and living in a world where they control upwards of 10 percent of its wealth, as they do today.[17]

Fitzgerald may succumb to scapegoating, but he nevertheless offers a guide to a world created by such an unequal distribution of wealth. To put it another way, my concern is not with the wealthy per se but how their habits—what they wear, how they treat others, and so on—shape our habits. We live in our world, but we also live in theirs. In the first chapter of the novel, Nick describes his small house as "an eyesore." But it was an eye-sore, he observes, among the mansions of Long Island that offered, as he put it, "the consoling proximity of millionaires."[18] Nick jokes, but I take his joke as a motive for this book, which is that the proximity of millionaires is not always consoling. It is often invidious, and not just for those who do not have wealth but for those who do. There is always a bigger house, always a bigger mansion, and always a second mansion.

II

Before closing this Introduction, I should say a word about

how I discuss the novel's four themes of clothes, waste, bonds, and race.

Like most literature, indeed like most writing, *The Great Gatsby* did not flawlessly emerge from the pen of its author. It went through multiple drafts. In 1924, Fitzgerald sent a typewritten copy of the manuscript to his editor at Scribner's, Maxwell Perkins. That draft does not survive, but the handwritten manuscript that served as the basis for it does. Based on suggestions Perkins gave, Fitzgerald revised the first draft. He titled the new draft "Trimalchio," a reference to a character in the Roman work *Satyricon* who shares many of the same traits as Gatsby: humble beginnings, new money, extravagant parties. Scribner's sent that draft back to Fitzgerald to proofread. Fitzgerald, however, did much more than proofread. He revised—at times simply rewrote—that manuscript and created the novel he chose to call *The Great Gatsby*.

It is fascinating to watch Fitzgerald across these generations of manuscripts. You witness what he keeps, what he adds, what he drops, and what he changes. Working backwards from the final draft reveals what Fitzgerald wanted *The Great Gatsby* to do, much like mapping the structure of the human brain reveals how it changed to suit its various purposes. The handwritten manuscript and the "Trimalchio" draft have been published, and I recommend reading them if you want to follow Fitzgerald along and achieve a fuller understanding of the novel.[19]

That said, in this book I mostly stick to the final draft of *The Great Gatsby*, the text of the 1925 first edition. This version is the one Fitzgerald wanted people to read, and this version is the one people will have read or will read.

Finally, I know that too many methodical investigations of a passage from a work of literature can bore readers. I have, as a result, tried to limit what in my world we call close readings.

Yet I also feel compelled to demonstrate how we—literary critics and literature professors—do what we do. The economy may have recovered from the Great Recession of 2008, but the humanities in general—and the discipline of English in particular—never did. If current trends continue, we risk losing not just a way to discuss works of literature but, equally important, a way to attend to language. As I announce to my students at the beginning of virtually every class I teach, if you are not using language, language is using you. And that, I add, is a recipe for political manipulation, regardless of which end of the political spectrum you start from.

Those who teach literature—and those who write books about literature—have a responsibility to help students and readers adopt a different attitude toward language. That requires an occasional microscopic attention to words and sentences. It is the least tribute we can pay to the extraordinary uses of language in our novels and poems, especially when those words and sentences, as the ones in *The Great Gatsby* do, offer insight into their world as well as ours.

III

One of my favorite passages in *The Great Gatsby* comes when the principal characters—Tom, Daisy, Jordan, Nick, and Gatsby—decide to drive to Manhattan to flee a burning late-summer day. Gatsby and Daisy have another motive, however, which is to deliver the news to Tom that he and Daisy intend to start a new life together. Gatsby and Nick are waiting in the driveway for everyone else to appear when Nick remarks that Daisy has "an indiscreet voice. It's full of . . ." But he cannot finish the thought. "It's full of money," Gatsby says, decisively, as though for the first time he recognizes the source of his desire for Daisy.[20] He loves Daisy the person, yes, but he also loves what Daisy represents, which is wealth and the life of wealth that, as the son of "shiftless and unsuccessful farm people," Gatsby could only dream of.

Like Daisy, our culture often speaks with a voice full of money. Buy this, and by buying this, be that. Or, failing that, risk becoming this. It behooves us to listen to those voices but to listen critically, so that, unlike Gatsby, we do not sacrifice ourselves to their song.

CHAPTER ONE

What to Wear in *The Great Gatsby*

It makes me sad because I've never seen such—such beautiful shirts before.

—DAISY BUCHANAN

An outfit called Rosé Lifestyle organizes annual Gatsby parties in New York City, Las Vegas, Los Angeles, Dallas, and Miami. In New York, general admission tickets start at $125, but $750 will get you a table for two on the floor. Those with deeper pockets can buy places at the Jay Gatsby Table, which start at $2,000 for a table of four. The party has a dress code: "Men are invited to come in black tie, while women are requested to arrive in flapper fashion." "The dress code is mandatory," the website adds, which is somewhat at odds with the less compulsory "invitation" extended to men to come in black tie and the "request" made of women to arrive in flapper fashion. But that is how dress codes work. They are voluntary until you violate them.[1]

For many people, black tie and flapper dresses epitomize *The Great Gatsby*, whether novel, film, or party. Yet one of the things that stands out about the novel is how often characters struggle to decipher the dress code. To get past the bouncer at a Gatsby party, you only have to follow the dress code for one night, and the code is simple: black tie and flapper dress. Someone has translated it for you. In *The Great Gatsby* the novel, the dress code is much more complicated, and it involves not just wearing the right clothes but also adopting the right attitude toward clothes. These habits are a lot to get right, and not everyone does. The title character, Gatsby, has the right attitude toward clothes but occasionally wears the wrong ones. Tom's mistress, Myrtle, is accumulating the right wardrobe but still learning the right attitude toward it. Their problems start when each, neither to the manner born, tries to mimic the rich. Gatsby does a better impression than Myrtle, but both ultimately fail. The novel does resemble a Gatsby party, though, in that its dress code is mandatory, even though the stakes are far higher. Both of the characters who violate it end up dead.

The dress codes in *The Great Gatsby* matter because in them we can gain a new perspective on our clothes. How do we decide what to wear? How does which social class we come from, and which social class we aspire to, influence those decisions? Do we, like Myrtle and Gatsby, try to mimic the rich? If so, how well do we succeed? And at what cost?

I

In 1924, a year before *The Great Gatsby* appeared, F. Scott Fitzgerald published an article in the *Baltimore American* with the title "What Kind of Husbands Do 'Jimmies' Make?" (The essay would appear elsewhere under the title "Our Irresponsible Rich.") Fitzgerald uses "Jimmy" as a catch-all term for a young man who comes from a wealthy family and lives a life of complete dissipation.[2] Because Fitzgerald uses the term "leisure class" in that article, many have speculated that he knew Thorstein Veblen's 1899 treatise, *The Theory of the Leisure Class*. Whether Veblen directly or indirectly influenced Fitzgerald, he left his fingerprints all over *The Great Gatsby*.

Veblen started from the anodyne premise that wealth distinguished—for the better—those who had it from those who did not, and those who did not have it invariably envied those who did. It was not enough to possess wealth, however. One had to signal their wealth through various stratagems. The wealthy could demonstrate how their wealth freed them from labor, what Veblen called "conspicuous leisure." Here one might think of Tom Buchanan, a "Jimmy" who has never worked a day in his life and has given no thought whatsoever to a profession. Instead, he tends his polo ponies, reads pseudo-intellectual books about race, seduces working-class women, and so on. These efforts require labor, of a sort, but they do not produce anything in the way that, say, a farmer grows wheat or a factory worker makes widgets. Indeed, Tom is so averse to work that he even gets someone else, George Wilson, to kill Gatsby.

Conspicuous leisure may not impress today as much as it did one hundred years ago. Our culture values conspicuous work as much as it does conspicuous leisure. As Tesla founder Elon Musk put it, "Work like hell. I mean you just have to put in 80- to 100-hour weeks every week."[3] Musk exaggerates, but only slightly. A 2018 Harvard study calculated that CEOs work 62.5 hours per week.[4] Even so, conspicuous leisure—or the signs of it—have not disappeared entirely. Witness, for example, the brisk trade in yachts and the gravity with which the wealthy undertake self-care.

Veblen thought the rich had another tactic for advertising their wealth and earning the esteem of others, which he called "conspicuous consumption." Consider the humble Casio F-91W-1 wristwatch. It tells the time. It has a stopwatch. It indicates the date. It knows how many days each month has so you do not need to change the date at the end of the month. It lights up in the dark. It will last for seven years before it needs a new battery. It fulfills virtually every function a watch should. It retails for $22.95. In 2023, I paid $17.99—it was on sale—for mine. By contrast, an entry-level Rolex costs $6,400 and it, well, it tells the time. (By the time you read this, the price will have increased by another $500 or $1,000.) Rolex does guarantee that its watch will run to within minus two to plus two seconds per day, which means that at most it will gain or lose 60 seconds per month. Yet Casio promises that its watch will lose or gain no more than 30 seconds per month.

So why do people buy Rolexes? One rationale is that a Rolex is more beautiful than the Casio. As someone who loves watches, I can vouch for that. One is made of cheap plastic and the other of what Rolex calls "Oystersteel." (Do not ask.) But Veblen quickly dismisses the argument. For him, what we call beauty is really just costliness disguised as beauty. Note that Veblen does not think that only expensive objects can be beautiful. After all, a sharpened pencil is one of the most beautiful objects in the world. But Veblen does think that expensive objects are beautiful because they are expensive. Their true value lies in proclaiming that you can buy a Rolex, that you have wealth to spare.

At the crossroads of conspicuous leisure and conspicuous consumption lie clothes. Veblen devotes an entire chapter to them. As with a Rolex, expensive clothes announce the wealth of those who wear them. Poke around websites like Hi-Consumption, Farfetch, and MyTheresa and, unless you are more worldly than I, you will be astonished at how much ordinary articles of clothing can cost. A plain white t-shirt from Ami Paris goes for $215, from Thom Browne for $270, and from Brunello Cuccinelli for $625.

Clothes can signal wealth in another way, not through their

expense but through how well (or poorly) they lend themselves to doing work. Some clothes make it all but impossible for those who wear them to perform manual labor. Try imagining a man in a top hat mining coal or a woman in a dress with an absurdly long train waiting tables. For clothes to signal wealth and leisure, they have to remain free from the perception that those who wear them work. "It goes without saying," Veblen observes, "that no apparel can be considered elegant, or even decent, if it shows the effect of manual labor on the part of the wearer."

If Fitzgerald did not in fact crib from Veblen, he nevertheless arrived at the same theory of the leisure class that Veblen did. Daisy cannot marry Gatsby because he is poor. Daisy does marry Tom because he is rich. And Tom trumpets his wealth by buying Daisy a string of pearls that costs $350,000, which would be just over six million dollars today. He has also mastered conspicuous leisure. He wastes his time playing polo and strutting around in polo clothes. There is nothing inconspicuous about Tom.

For Gatsby to win Daisy back, he too must make his wealth conspicuous. Unlike Tom, he cannot win on conspicuous leisure alone. Throughout the novel, Gatsby is called away by his butler, who informs him that Philadelphia or Detroit or Chicago is on the phone. Gatsby must take the calls, which shows that he has not fully arrived in the land of conspicuous leisure. By contrast, no one asks anything of Tom. Gatsby makes up for working, though, through astonishingly conspicuous consumption.

He buys a garish mansion. He buys a garish car. He buys a hydroplane, which is garish in and of itself. He throws enormous, decadent parties. More intimately, he announces his newfound wealth by the clothes he wears.

Gatsby understands better than anyone how clothes accompany—even enable—the rise from poverty to plenty. His ascent from "shiftless and unsuccessful farm people" begins when he rows out on Lake Superior to warn a millionaire, Dan Cody, that he has anchored his yacht on an especially treacherous stretch of water. Cody takes Gatsby on as a "steward, mate, skipper, secretary, and even jailor"—Cody drinks too much—and his first gift to the young man is to take him to Duluth and buy him "a blue coat, six pair of white duck trousers and a yachting cap."[5]

The gambler and racketeer Meyer Wolfsheim plays a similar role in outfitting Gatsby. Wolfsheim gives Gatsby his start in business, which includes buying him a new wardrobe. Wolfsheim, who wears human molars as cufflinks, clothes Gatsby in a less aggressive but no less fashionable style.

The only time clothes do not matter is when everyone wears the same ones. When Gatsby meets Daisy in Louisville before shipping out to France, he hides behind, as Nick writes, "the invisible cloak of his uniform." Because all the soldiers who fancy Daisy wear a uniform, none of them can distinguish themselves from each other by the clothes they wear. Gatsby, who we later learn has literally no other clothes, can take advantage of the situation. Indeed, he "takes" Daisy "under false pretenses."[6] Gatsby does not lie, but he does let Daisy believe that he comes from the same world of wealth and privilege that she does. He can do so because the uniformity of military uniforms obscures his poverty.

When Gatsby reunites with Daisy five years later, after she has rejected him because of his poverty, he strategically leads with his clothes. When they meet at Nick's bungalow, Gatsby arrives dressed, somewhat comically, in precious metals. He wears "a white flannel suit, silver shirt and gold-colored tie."[7] Nothing impresses Daisy, though, quite like Gatsby's shirts. After their reunion, Gatsby leads Daisy and Nick on a tour of his mansion, and they stop in his bedroom so he can show off his wardrobe. Daisy responds—the best word is erotically—to his shirts, which are "piled like bricks in stacks a dozen high." The whole passage, narrated by Nick, bears quoting. Bragging that he has "a man in England who buys me clothes," Gatsby

> took out a pile of shirts and began throwing them, one by one, before us, shirts of sheer linen and thick silk and fine flannel, which lost their folds as they fell and covered the table in many-colored disarray. While we admired he brought more and the soft rich heap mounted higher—shirts with stripes and scrolls and plaids in coral and apple-green and lavender and faint orange, with monograms of Indian blue. Suddenly, with a strained sound, Daisy bent her head into the shirts and began to cry stormily.

Figure 1.1 "The advertisement of the man."

"They're such beautiful shirts," she sobbed, her voice muffled in the thick folds. "It makes me sad because I've never seen such—such beautiful shirts before."[8]

The adjective "rich" in "the soft rich heap" of shirts means plentiful or abundant, but it also means just plain rich. Gatsby has invested his money in shirts, and his investment pays off: Daisy melts. Her reaction passes from esteem to worship.

Unsurprisingly, Daisy later associates Gatsby with shirts—or the collars of shirts, anyway. In blistering heat, at a lunch with the whole roster of characters, Daisy feebly compares Gatsby to a well-dressed fiction. "'You always look so cool,'" she tells him. "'You resemble the advertisement of the man . . . You know the advertisement of the man.'"[9] Daisy probably has in mind the ubiquitous advertisements of the

Arrow-Collar man, the unlikely heartthrob of the first decades of the twentieth century (see Figure 1.1).

Although Daisy cannot remember the name of the man or the article of clothing he sells, she is right to compare Gatsby to an advertisement, because Gatsby is selling himself, or an image of himself. Whether Daisy grasps it or not, she has not fallen in love with Gatsby but with the billboard of himself that he has created. A cynic might conclude she does not love Gatsby but his shirts.[10]

If clothes make Gatsby, they also contribute to his undoing. Tom is never taken in by Gatsby, and after he and Daisy attend one of his parties, he investigates where Gatsby comes from and how he made his money. He never learns where Gatsby comes from, but he does learn where his money comes from, and where he does *not* come from. Gatsby claims to have attended Oxford College. On the car ride to Manhattan, Jordan and Nick confirm his story. Nick has seen a picture of Gatsby at Oxford. But Tom does not buy it, and his reasons are sartorial. "An Oxford man!" Tom roars. "Like hell he is! He wears a pink suit."[11]

Unlike Daisy, Tom does not fall for the advertisement Gatsby has clumsily made of himself. Tom knows that graduates of Oxford would never wear something as loud as a pink suit. But Gatsby does not know that. He has a lot of clothes, but not the taste to wear the right ones. His party may lead Tom to investigate Gatsby, and his wife falling in love with Gatsby may lead Tom to confront Gatsby with what he has learned, but it is the clothes Gatsby wears that for Tom confirm that Gatsby is a fraud: "Oxford, New Mexico," Tom adds, "or something like that."[12]

It makes sense, for Fitzgerald and his readers, that this scene precedes the climax of the novel in a suite of the Plaza Hotel, when Tom reveals to Daisy the crooked ways Gatsby has made his money and, thus, what she will attach herself to if she follows through on her halfhearted assertion that she intends to leave Tom for Gatsby. She would be his partner in crime. She would leave her fashionable neighborhood on Long Island for the vulgar one where Gatsby lives. She would share his pink suit.

Gatsby comes close, ever so close, to bringing off the role of the wealthy gentleman in the play he puts on for Daisy. He has bought a lot of clothes, more than he could ever wear, and none besmirched by labor. For just one scene, when he appears in the wrong costume, a pink suit, the performance fails.

II

Gatsby can make a good claim to it, but no character illustrates the significance of clothes as much as Myrtle, Tom's mistress. When she tells Nick how she and Tom met, her story focuses on what Tom wore. She first encounters Tom on the train into Manhattan. He sits across from her, and the first thing she notices is his suit (dress) and his shoes (patent-leather). In the station, Myrtle does not feel Tom against her arm but his shirt (white). Basically, she has been seduced by a mannequin.

A Rotten Crowd

Impressed by what Tom wears, Myrtle devotes the most thought and the most effort to what she wears. She first appears in the garage-slash-gas station that George owns in a spotted dress of dark blue crepe-de-chine. (Don't let the French fool you. Crepe-de-chine does not mean Chinese pancake. It refers to a fabric that somehow reminded the French of China.) Later, at a party in the small apartment in the Bronx that Tom rents for her, Myrtle changes into "an elaborate afternoon dress of cream-colored chiffon." Myrtle does not just change her dress; the dress changes her. Instead of the fiery "vitality" that emanates from her at the garage, now she adopts "an impressive hauteur."[13] Suddenly, and without any self-consciousness, she becomes a snob. She criticizes men who only "think of money," and she complains about a shiftless elevator boy whom she sends out to get ice. "These people! You have to keep after them all the time."[14]

As much as she cares about clothes, both in her appraisal of others and herself, she knows that to pull off an impression of a privileged woman, she has to pretend not to care about clothes. When her neighbor at the apartment compliments her dress, she dismisses the compliment. "It's just a crazy old thing," she says. "I just slip it on sometimes when I don't care what I look like."[15] Later, she promises to give her neighbor the dress since "I've got to get another one tomorrow."[16] Myrtle wants to sound like someone—someone rich—who could casually give away an expensive dress because she

36

could just as easily acquire a new one the next day, and the day after that, and the day after that.[17]

If Gatsby gets the attitude right and the clothes wrong, Myrtle gets the clothes right—Tom buys them for her and promises to buy more—but struggles with the attitude. As Tom and Daisy intuitively know, to dress well means not to care overly much about how you or others dress. But Myrtle cannot pull off that indifference. Clothes obviously matter far too much to her.[18] For her, clothes are not what you put on but what they reveal and how they change your very being. As Nick describes her after she has put on her new dress, "Her laughter, her gestures, her assertions became more violently affected moment by moment."[19]

Of the two, Gatsby and Myrtle, the latter is the more pathetic. Gatsby may someday learn that someone who attended Oxford would never wear a pink suit. But Myrtle will always struggle with the insouciance required of the wealthy. Poor but with pretensions to wealth, she is like the mongrel puppy Tom buys for her outside of Penn Station when they arrive in Manhattan. As she cruelly says of her husband, she too has no "breeding."

II

So, are we a Gatsby or a Myrtle? Do we too try to mimic the wealthy in dress and attitude? According to a host of sociologists, amateur and professional, we do.

According to them, the wealthy adopt new fashions created

for them by celebrated designers. Then, gradually, those styles "trickle down" to the less wealthy, each class abandoning them as the class lower on the totem pole embraces them. The French sociologist Pierre Bourdieu offered the pithiest description of this dynamic: "When the miniskirt reaches the mining villages of northern France, it's time to start all over again."[20]

The better-known version comes from the film *The Devil Wears Prada*, when Meryl Streep, doing her best Anna Wintour impersonation, dissects the anatomy of the "lumpy blue sweater"—actually "cerulean"—worn by the Anne Hathaway character:

> You're . . . blithely unaware of the fact that, in 2002, Oscar de la Renta did a collection of cerulean gowns, and then I think it was Yves Saint Laurent, wasn't it, who showed cerulean military jackets? And then cerulean quickly showed up in the collections of eight different designers. Then it filtered down through the department stores, and then trickled on down into some tragic Casual Corner where you, no doubt, fished it out of some clearance bin.[21]

What both Streep-slash-Wintour describes is what has come to be called "fast fashion." Designers introduce haute couture styles to the catwalk, which the wealthy buy at exclusive boutiques. Soon enough, designers at other brands adopt and adapt the styles, which are sent abroad for mass production.

The clothes return on container ships to be displayed and sold at Topshop, H & M, Zara, and the like, eventually making their way down the fashion food chain to Target, Walmart, and Kohl's. Whereas the cycle used to take years—designs that appeared last winter would appear in stores the following winter—now the dynamic has accelerated, not measured in years but months and even weeks.

Regardless of the timeline, and regardless of whether we know it or not, what we wear often derives from what the wealthy wore. Gatsby and Myrtle may wear the real thing, and we may wear knockoffs, but we all strive, as Jay Z once put it, to look like wealth.[22]

That dynamic applies even today, when it may seem as though many of the wealthiest individuals in America shun fashion. Think of Mark Zuckerberg and his hoodies, Bill Gates and his V-neck sweaters, or the crypto-grifter Sam Bankman-Fried and his cargo shorts and t-shirts. And for those who do not eschew fashion, there are those who exemplify the latest trend in fashion, quiet luxury or stealth wealth. Those who adopt this style do not worry about demonstrating their wealth to those below them. As one influencer described the approach, "I'm so rich, I don't even need to tell you how rich I am."[23] Instead, like a secret handshake, the stealthy wealthy aspire to signal their wealth to their fellow inhabitants of the top 1 percent but could not care less about the 99 percent. Hence the $625 T-shirt from Brunello Cuccinelli. To the untrained eye, it looks like a white T-shirt. To the well-trained eye, its cut and material look like what French cuffs and a silk pocket square did a century ago. [24]

Yet the trend toward quiet luxury and stealth wealth only reinforces the point that Bourdieu made fifty years ago. Any number of guides on Tik Tok will help you and me achieve the quiet luxury look. If we start to achieve that look too well, if it becomes too loud, you can take bets on how long it will be until the wealthy adopt a different style. To borrow from Bourdieu, when stealth wealth reaches H&M and the suburbs of Pittsburgh—and it has—it's time to start all over again.

We resemble Gatsby and Myrtle not just in the design and aspirations of our clothes but also in the volume of them. Until very recently, only the wealthy had more clothes than they could wear. Now, thanks to fast fashion, almost everyone does. In 2018, the latest year for which we have data, Americans bought nearly seventy pieces of clothing apiece. Put differently, the average American buys a new article of clothing every five days. [25] Households now spend $1,890 for clothes, which consumes 2.5 percent of their income. [26] By contrast, in 1960 Americans purchased roughly twenty-five articles of clothing per year. [27] Doing so cost them $695 per household, or 10.4 percent of their income. [28] Adjusted for inflation, that $695 is $5,900 in 2018 dollars. (See Figure 1.2.) To put it plainly, clothes used to be very expensive. Or, perhaps more to the point, clothes are now very cheap. Either way, it constitutes a triumph of marketing—or fashion or the desire for variation or all three—that as clothes got cheaper,

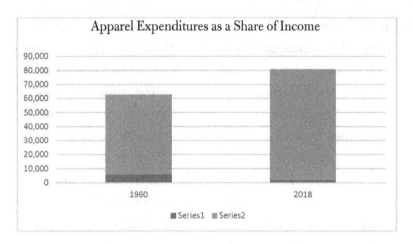

Figure 1.2. The number on the left displays household income.

Americans bought more and more of them rather than buying the same amount and pocketing the difference between what clothes cost then and what they cost now.

How did we go from purchasing fewer clothes for more money to purchasing more clothes for less money? In a word, globalization. (In a second word, automation.) In 1960, 1,233,000 Americans worked in garment factories and made 95 percent of the clothing their fellow Americans wore.[29] In 2010, 150,000 Americans worked in garment factories and made just 2.5 percent of the clothes Americans wore.[30] The numbers have only shrunk since.

Where did all the work go? Asia. Like gravity, low wages pulled manufacturing from West to East.[31] An American garment worker makes four times what a Chinese worker does, eleven times what a Dominican worker does, and thirty-eight times what a Bangladeshi worker does.[32] In 2013, the *New York Times* broke down how much it cost to make a deluxe hoodie in the United States or in Asia. The difference, $38.10 versus $31.40, derives almost entirely from labor. Clothing companies paid $17.00 in hourly wages to make a hoodie in the United States. They spent $5.50 to make it in Asia.[33] The difference between $38.10 and $31.40 may not seem like much, but it adds up. No one knows exactly how many hoodies Americans buy each year, but estimates put it north of 50 million.[34] In which case, the difference between making hoodies in the United States rather than Asia runs to hundreds of millions of dollars.

Like Myrtle, who gives away the dress she wears today because she will get a new one tomorrow, fast, cheap fashion enables Americans to give away their old clothes to make room for new ones. In 2018, *The Saturday Evening Post* estimated that Americans throw away 81 pounds of clothing per year.[35] Our biggest export, by volume, is used clothing.[36] We may not belong to the leisure class, but we waste clothes like they do.

Whereas Americans used to have few clothes and good manufacturing jobs, now we have many clothes and few good manufacturing jobs. In 2018, *Forbes* estimated that five of the world's 55 wealthiest people owned fashion companies.[37]

What we buy and where it comes from has enriched a handful of individuals. It has also impoverished the roughly one out of six people on Earth who work in the garment industry.[38] True, many of those people were poor before they entered sweatshops, but only the most optimistic among us can celebrate people moving from extreme poverty to ordinary poverty. If Veblen is right that what we wear signals who we are, then what does what we wear today reveal about us? In plain English, it reveals we are in thrall to changing fashions and whatever the wealthy happened to wear last year, last month, or last week.

One of my favorite scenes in *The Great Gatsby* is when all the characters drive to Manhattan because they are hot. There they decide, for no good reason, to take a room at the Plaza Hotel. While they argue about it, Nick, looking backwards on the scene, writes: "I have a sharp physical memory that, in the course of [the argument], my underwear kept climbing like a damp snake around my legs and intermittent beads of sweat raced cool across my back."[39] It is one of the few times that Nick, the narrator of the novel, refers to what he wears. But his simile is apt. As some but not all of the characters in the novel discover, clothes *are* like a damp snake. If you are not careful, they can climb around your body and, like a snake, be just as constricting to yourself and others.

CHAPTER TWO

Among the Ash Heaps and Millionaires

> But I wanted to leave things in order and not just trust that
> obliging and indifferent sea to sweep my refuse away.
>
> —NICK CARRAWAY, ON CLOSING HIS
> RELATIONSHIP WITH JORDAN BAKER

Can a book change a landscape? If ever a book did, it was *The Great Gatsby*.

The previous chapter explored how clothes in *The Great Gatsby* followed a Veblen-like logic of conspicuous leisure and, still more so, conspicuous consumption. For Veblen, what unites conspicuous leisure and conspicuous consumption, beyond the need for visibility, is waste. To conspicuously consume, the wealthy need to advertise that they can waste resources. So they spend hundreds of thousands of dollars on a car when a thirty-thousand dollar one would do, or, as Gatsby does for the parties he throws, spend grotesque amounts of money on food and alcohol.

But waste informs *The Great Gatsby* in ways other than conspicuous consumption, nowhere more so than in the valley of ashes that characters pass through on their way to Manhattan and on whose outskirts George and Myrtle Wilson live. In these ashes, we can foresee the culture of waste that has irrevocably harmed our own world and threatens to harm it still more. Although no one is innocent, including us for mimicking them, the wealthy, just as they did in the realm of clothes, bear more responsibility for this culture of waste than do others. The story starts not on Long Island, where *The Great Gatsby* largely takes place, but in Brooklyn. It ends, like the novel, on Long Island, but it ends with one extraordinarily ambitious reader, the urban planner Robert Moses.

I

By 1898, when Brooklyn joined the other boroughs to form New York City, it had already run out of room for its garbage and the tons of ashes generated by the coal its residents burned to heat their homes. Until 1906, the Street Cleaning Department had used horse-drawn carts to collect garbage and ash and haul it to dumps, some as far as ten miles away. Or, if that required too much effort, they simply threw it in the ocean. Because of this laborious system, the *New York Times* reported in 1907, "It was a common thing in any street in the borough to see barrels running over with ash standing for days and sometimes a week in front of houses."[1]

Enter the Brooklyn Ash Removal Company and its treasurer, the Tammany Hall insider John "Fishhooks" McCarthy. Accounts vary, but his nickname is thought to refer to how, whenever a bill appeared, his hands, like fishhooks, got caught in his pockets, making it impossible for him to pay.[2] In 1906, in a sweetheart deal that nevertheless smelled as bad as the offal it disposed of, his Brooklyn Ash Removal Company won a contract with the city to gather its ashes and street sweepings (a pretty word for horse manure), haul them by trolley to a railway station, and then send them to what the *Times* called the "the waste lands around Coney Island," where they were unceremoniously dumped. But all that waste— ash, manure, garbage—did not go to waste. They turned the "waste land"—in reality, ecologically vital marsh lands—of Coney Island into valuable real estate, which was owned by none other than the Brooklyn Ash Removal Company. This was nice work if you could get it. As the *Times* reported, "The coal brought to [Brooklyn] out of the Pennsylvania hills finds its way in its reduced state as taken from the stoves and furnaces to her tide-washed meadows, to convert them into sites for new homes," adding, "The scheme is also making wealth for those who own the once valueless marsh lands."[3]

By 1910, the Brooklyn Ash Removal Company had buried the meadows of Coney Island beneath layers of ash. (Look at a map today and you will notice that Coney Island is no longer

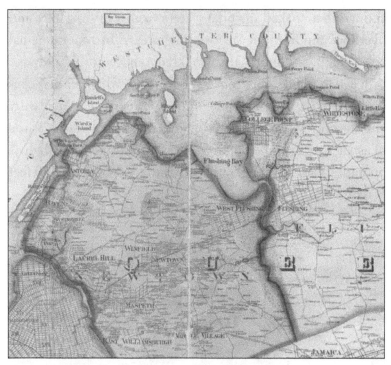

Figure 2.1. 1859 map of Queens County. Flushing Bay is in the center. The Flushing River divides what was Newton County (on the left) from Flushing County (on the right). The marshlands are marked with black dots to the east and west of the Flushing River. Manhattan lies west of narrow Roosevelt Island (then Rockwell Island) in the East River.[4]

an island.) So, McCarthy and the Brooklyn Ash Company shifted operations to the wastelands of Flushing Creek in Queens which, it so happened, it also owned (see Figure 2.1).

Since the glaciers retreated roughly 10,000 years ago, the land around Flushing Creek had been marshland, a low-lying sponge that soaked up tidal waters from Flushing Bay and overflow rain from the surrounding areas.[5] In a monumental act of ecological hubris, the Brooklyn Ash Removal Company proceeded to fill it in. From 1910 to 1934, when the city canceled its contract with the company,[6] Fishhooks McCarthy and his crew deposited an estimated fifty million cubic yards of ash across its three hundred acres. Mounds rose as high as 30 and 40 feet and one, dubbed Mount Corona, rose 90 feet (Figure 2.2).[7]

Figure 2.2. Mount Corona. The photograph was taken in 1934, after the city canceled its contract with the Brooklyn Ash Removal Company.

In 1922, F. Scott Fitzgerald moved to Long Island and commuted to Manhattan by car and train. His path skirted the Corona Dump, which would play a crucial role in the novel he was writing at the time. In the second chapter of *The Great Gatsby*, Nick famously describes what he called "a valley of ashes":

> About halfway between West Egg and New York the motor road hastily joins the railroad and runs beside it for a quarter of a mile, so as to shrink away from a certain desolate area of land. This is a valley of ashes—a fantastic farm where ashes grow like wheat into ridges and hills and grotesque gardens; where ashes take the forms of houses and chimneys and rising smoke and, finally, with a transcendent effort, of ash-grey men, who move dimly and already crumbling through the powdery air. Occasionally a line of grey cars crawls along an invisible track, gives out a ghastly creak, and comes to rest, and immediately the ash-grey men swarm up with leaden spades and stir up an impenetrable cloud, which screens their obscure operations from your sight.[8]

The beauty of this passage, if you can speak of beauty in it, is how the ashes in the valley of ashes come alive. A "certain desolate area of land" turns into "a fantastic farm where ashes grow like wheat." The ashes turn into a landscape—ridges, hills, and gardens—that encompass the farm. Finally, the landscape gives birth to humans, first their houses and

Figure 2.3. "Occasionally a line of grey cars crawls along an invisible track, gives out a ghastly creak, and comes to rest."

chimneys but then the "ash-grey men," who appear dimly and, like the geographical formations the ash creates, already crumbling. The final sentence is the most disturbing. It could easily belong in one of the circles of hell Dante describes in *The Inferno*. Its verbs invoke disquieting creatures: the grey cars "crawl" like a snake; they give out a "ghastly creak" like a ghost; and the men "swarm" the cars like flies to a carcass (Figure 2.3). Eventually, all disappears behind a veil of ashes.

New York Route 25A, which still skirts Flushing Bay to the north, is the road characters in *The Great Gatsby* likely took from Long Island to Manhattan, though some have guessed that the road crossing the river at the bottom of the photo (Figure 2.4) is more likely, especially since the route goes through rather than around the valley. Either way, ashes.[9]

So no wonder the road shrinks away. The haunting descrip-

Figure 2.4. 1924 Aerial photo of Flushing Bay; Flushing River, which curves east then southwest of the bay; and the valley of ashes.

tion invokes "The Order of the Burial of the Dead," the common prayer in which a priest casts earth upon a corpse and says (or sings), "I commend thy soul to God the Father Almighty, and thy body to the ground, earth to earth, ashes to ashes, dust to dust." That prayer invokes Genesis 2:7, where God "formed man of the dust," to which his body would return upon death. Finally, the valley of ashes recalls Psalm 23, which begins "Yea, though I walk through the valley of the shadow of death. . . ." The difference is that unlike the Psalm, the valley of ashes offers no consolation, no Christ-like shepherd who will comfort us and lead us to fear no evil. Instead, we are on our own.[10]

Like the nauseating smell of the Corona Dump, which wafted to adjacent neighborhoods and forced residents to keep their windows closed, especially in the summer, the dust in the "valley of ashes" does not stay put.[11] In the novel, not only does it invoke death; it figuratively brings death.

In the opening paragraphs of the book, Nick declares, implausibly, that "No—Gatsby turned out all right at the end." Rather, it is "what preyed on Gatsby, what foul dust floated in the wake of his dreams" that Nick blames for the tragedy he will recount.[12]

Readers sometimes hurry past these lines, but they reward closer attention. Gatsby is preyed on, which is a clear enough image, but what preys on him and floats behind him—the dust—makes less sense. At first glance, when Nick uses the word "wake," it seems like he describes the dust in terms of water. Like a boat through the sea, perhaps like the one the Dutch sailors arrive in at the conclusion of the novel, Gatsby and his dreams leave a wake behind them. Then the dust, which floats, preys on Gatsby and his dream, like a gannet or tern that dives into water for fish. That George kills Gatsby in his swimming pool, that he falls prey to George, underscores that reading.[13] So too does the use of "wake" in funerary rites. At the end of the novel, Nick will keep a lonely vigil beside Gatsby's body.

In any case, dust comes for Gatsby. All these images—dust, dreams, water, prey—converge in the next to last chapter, when Gatsby realizes that Daisy will not come to him:

He must have felt that he had lost the old warm world, paid a high price for living too long with a single dream. He must have looked up at an unfamiliar sky through frightening leaves and shivered as he found what a grotesque thing a rose is and how raw the sunlight was upon the scarcely created grass. A new world, material without being real, where poor ghosts, breathing dreams like air, drifted fortuitously about . . . like that ashen, fantastic figure gliding toward him through the amorphous trees.[14]

The ashen, fantastic figure gliding toward him is George Wilson, who will kill Gatsby and himself. And Wilson, who murders Gatsby, is dust personified. "A white ashen dust," Fitzgerald writes of him early in the novel, "veiled his dark suit and his pale hair as it veiled everything in the vicinity."[15]

Here and elsewhere in the novel, Fitzgerald has arranged his ashes and dust just so. The motif appears over and over again:

- In the second chapter, when Myrtle is at her liveliest, she is described as "smouldering."[16] Later in the chapter, she includes "one of those cute little ashtrays where you touch a spring" on the "list of all things [she's] got to get."[17] After Daisy runs her over, Nick observes that Myrtle "knelt in the road and mingled her thick, dark blood with the dust."[18] And riding through the ash heaps to Manhattan, Nick will cross to the other side of the train to avoid seeing "a curious crowd around there all day with little boys searching for dark spots in the dust."[19]

- In the penultimate chapter, as Tom, Nick, and Jordan stop for gas, Gatsby and Daisy pass them on the way to Manhattan, "their car flash[ing] by us with a flurry of dust."[20] Daisy will soon kill someone in that dust (Myrtle) and Gatsby will be killed by someone from it (George).
- When Gatsby returns to his mansion after Daisy has forsaken him, he and Nick search for a cigarette—more ashes—and Nick observes "an inexplicable amount of dust everywhere."[21] Soon, the ashen figure of George will appear to spread the dust from mansion to owner.
- At the end of the novel, Tom tells Nick that Gatsby threw "'dust into your eyes, just like he did in Daisy's.'"[22] That is rich coming from Tom, who threw dust personified, George Wilson, at Gatsby.

Then there is this: As Nick and the gardener carry Gatsby's body to the mansion, the gardener spots Wilson's body "a little way off in the grass." "The holocaust," Nick observes, "was complete."[23] Prior to the Second World War, *holocaust* did not refer to the mass murder of Jews and other outsiders. It referred to wholesale destruction, usually by fire. Its etymology makes that clear. The word comes from the Greek *holos*, meaning "whole," and *kaustos*, meaning "burnt." The whole of it is burnt.

Seen through the dust, darkly, *The Great Gatsby* reads like an exercise in the waste of energy (coal), land (Flushing), and life (Myrtle, Gatsby, and George). One can read its famous ending many ways, and I will, but for now note that once developed, there is no returning to the "fresh, green breast of the new world" that "flowered once for Dutch sailors' eyes."[24] Like Tom, Daisy, and Jordan, whom Nick will call "a rotten crowd," the continent, like milk, has soured. Ashes cannot turn back into coal—nor garbage dumps back into marsh-land. Starting with the Dutch sailors, as the land is developed, it is simultaneously despoiled.

One of the titles Fitzgerald gave to his novel—he was never satisfied with any of them—was *Among the Ash Heaps and Millionaires*. The title juxtaposes landscape (ash heaps) and humans (millionaires), and its preposition, *Among*, implies more than just a spacial relationship between the two. It implies a shared world, one that includes both setting and character. And so it is. Or was. Until the city turned to its master builder to clean up the mess—a master builder whose reading of *The Great Gatsby* would inspire him to redeem the wasteland.

II

If you go looking for the valley of ashes today, you will find not ashes but a baseball stadium (Citi Field), a tennis center (home to the U.S. Open), two man-made lakes, an amusement park, and most disconcerting of all, a stainless-steel sculpture of the globe measuring 115 feet in diameter. There is also a zoo. In less than a decade, Flushing Meadows went from blight to blessing. In doing so, it embodied the decisions that would lead, step by step, to our own experiment in creating waste, and to the potentially catastrophic climate change we face as a result.

In 1934, New York City decided that it had lined the pockets of Fishhooks McCarthy long enough. It canceled its contract with the Brooklyn Ash Removal Company and started disposing of its own waste. But now it had a valley of ashes on its hands.[25]

Where others saw ashes, Robert Moses, the infamous urban planner, saw an opportunity. In 1932, Moses was appointed Commissioner of the New York City Parks Department, the perch from which he would oversee the remaking of the city for the next twenty-five years. In 1934, Moses added to his resumé when he was appointed chair of the Triborough Bridge Authority and salvaged that project from runaway costs and runaway incompetence. Unsatisfied by his bridges, Moses sought to build a parkway—what eventually became Grand Central Parkway—connecting the Queens–Wards Island span of the Triborough Bridge to the existing parkway of Eastern Long Island. (See Figure 2.5 for a contemporary view of the park.) The route, Moses wrote a few years later, "led inevitably along the Flushing Bay through the Flushing Meadow and the middle of the Corona Dump."[26] "This was the logical place for it," he added, "but only on the assumption that there was to be a general reclamation of the surrounding area." In the midst of the Great Depression, however, "there was no sign of money in the offing."[27]

Until, that is, what Moses called "a group of prominent citizens" wanted to hold a World's Fair in the city in 1939. Moses told the planners that "the Flushing Meadow was the only place in New York where they could get any cooperation from the Parks Department." Of course, Moses *was* the Parks Department, so Flushing Meadow it would be. Moses could not have cared less about a fair, which he dismissed as an exercise in "amusements and ballyhoo." For him, as he wrote in 1938, the "fair was the obvious bait for the reclamation of the meadow."[28] The fair would fund his ambitious plan to turn the Corona Dump into a park even larger than Central Park.

Strangely, and a little surprisingly, Moses often credited *The Great Gatsby* as part of his inspiration for remaking Flushing Meadow. In his 1938 article for *The Saturday Evening Post*, Moses immodestly described his heroic efforts to turn Flushing Meadow, as his title put it, "From Dump to Glory." In the same article, he quotes the "valley of ashes" paragraphs from Fitzgerald and says of *The Great Gatsby* that it "remained a good yarn even after the Depression had leveled off the moraine of gold deposited on the North Shore in the delirious Twenties."[29] Keep in mind that by 1938, the novel—and its author—had been all but forgotten, so much so that Moses had to summarize the plot for his readers: "It was a gaudy tale about a racketeer who tried to break into North Shore Long Island to be near a woman with whom he had enjoyed a fleeting romance."[30] In 1966, after scholars and readers had rediscovered Fitzgerald and *The Great Gatsby*,

Moses published a pamphlet, *The Saga of Flushing Meadow*, that described how "two World's Fairs had ushered in, at the very geographical and population center of New York, on the scene of a notorious ash dump, one of the very great municipal parks of our country."[31] The cover of the pamphlet depicts the aerial photograph of the site that Moses commissioned in 1934 before work began on the Corona Dump. Moses has labeled the photograph "The Valley of Ashes." And in 1974, Moses wrote a 3,500-word letter to *The New Yorker* after it published excerpts of the unflattering biography of him written by Robert Caro. In it, Moses bragged "of the huge task of reclaiming this fetid meadow blocked by the biggest ash dump in municipal history, so well described in 'The Great Gatsby.'"[32]

One can imagine a world in which, absent *The Great Gatsby*, there would be no Flushing Meadow Park. At the least, the park would have dropped down the list of urban planning priorities Moses kept.

In the 1974 letter, Moses defended himself from critics "who shout for rails and inveigh against rubber but admit that they live in the suburbs and that their wives are absolutely dependent on motor cars." Like it or not, he asserted, "We live in a motorized city."[33] (Alas, he was right.) If so, the 1939 World's Fair prepared the way for that motorized city. As part of the planning for the fair, Moses got his roads. Flushing Meadow was now bounded on three sides by highways: Whitestone Parkway (later the Van Wyck Expressway) to the

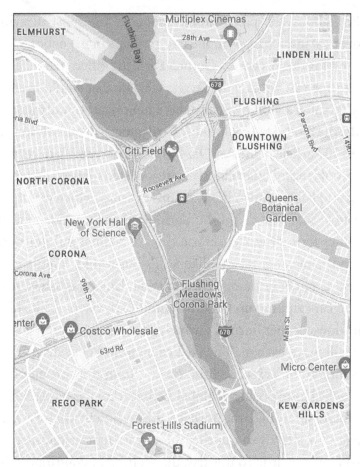

Figure 2.5 Flushing Meadows Corona Park today.

east; an expanded Union Turnpike to the south; and Grand Central Parkway to the west. Today, Flushing Meadow looks like a park circled and intersected by highways. (The Long Island Expressway bisects it like a crease in a sheet of paper.)

Throughout, the park contains some of the most dizzying cloverleaf interchanges in the city, perhaps in the country.

In Flushing Meadows Corona Park, the official name of the park, one can witness the layers of waste that would eventually threaten a motorized city and a motorized country alike—indeed, a motorized civilization. Coal mined in Pennsylvania, as the 1907 article in the *New York Times* observed, made its way to Brooklyn and other cities, where it heated houses and buildings and left behind millions of tons of ashes, which would lay waste to marshland. Yet the burning of coal would generate another form of waste, carbon dioxide, which did not leave behind a material residue like ashes but would cumulatively cause as much or more environmental damage as ashes. And those cars zipping up Grand Central Parkway past Flushing Meadows proper burned through gasoline that would generate still more carbon. The coal came from Pennsylvania, the gasoline from Texas, and the carbon from the consumption of each. Unsurprisingly, global carbon dioxide levels began to increase around the turn of the twentieth century and, except for a few years during the Great Depression, steadily swooped upward. To this day, the sector that contributes the most to greenhouse gases is transportation.[34]

In 2012, Hurricane Sandy would reveal everything that went wrong with the human engineering of Flushing Meadow. The burning of coal added carbon to the atmosphere. The burning of gasoline added still more. Both raised sea levels and warmed the ocean, making hurricanes stronger and more likely. And by turning Flushing Meadow into Flushing Meadows Corona Park, the city replaced a sponge that would soak up seawater into, effectively, a concrete slab, which like a shallow tub would fill up and overflow into the basements and first floors of houses and businesses in surrounding neighborhoods.[35]

You cannot pin this waste wholly on the wealthy, but they may deserve more of the blame than others. In 2019, the bottom 50 percent of earners in the United States generated a little less than 10 tons of carbon dioxide per capita. That same year, the top 10 percent produced 75 tons of carbon per person. Globally, the top 10 percent was responsible for nearly half of all carbon emissions. And the top one percent created 17 percent of all emissions.[36] In short, the wealthier the filthier, which makes sense. It is the wealthy that fly and buy the most.

If you believe, as I do, that the wealthy set the standard for consumption, which those below them aspire to and, as much as possible, adopt; and if you believe, as ecologically inclined economists do, that more and more consumption generates more and more waste; then it would seem that no small part of the environmental damage visited upon the earth in the century since *The Great Gatsby* was published traces back to the wealthy. Follow the money, and there you find the waste.

Indeed, you can read *The Great Gatsby* as an allegory of impending environmental catastrophe. The "death car" that kills Myrtle operates in a wasteland of ashes. The repurposing of that wasteland, its transformation from, as Robert Moses wrote, dump to glory, meant surrounding it on all sides by highways, which would exploit other forms of resources, namely oil refined into gasoline, which would generate the carbon dioxide that is heating up the earth at record and unsustainable levels.

On the surface, Flushing Meadows Corona Park looks more bucolic than when it was a valley of ashes. But from a longer perspective, it looks like another icon of waste.

All this waste can change how we read the last comments Nick offers about Tom and Daisy: "They were careless people," he writes. "They smashed up things and creatures and then retreated back into their money or their vast care-lessness or whatever it was that kept them together, and let other people clean up the mess they had made."[37] We are still cleaning up that mess. In many ways, we have not even begun.

CHAPTER THREE

"You're Selling Bonds, Aren't You, Old Sport?"

He used to be my best friend.
—GATSBY, SPEAKING OF DAN CODY

Despite its swooping, three-dimensional camerawork—or perhaps because of it—many critics left the 2013 film version of *The Great Gatsby* disappointed. One thing the film gets right, though, which the novel only suggests, comes early when Nick agrees to invite Daisy to his bungalow for tea so that Gatsby can ambush her after five years apart. Out of gratitude, Gatsby offers to repay Nick in the only language he speaks, which is money. He asks Nick, "You're selling bonds, aren't you, old sport?" When Nick acknowledges that he is, Gatsby invites him to share in some of his "little business on the side, a sort of sideline." Gatsby, Fitzgerald implies, deals in stolen bonds, and, since Nick has come to New York to sell bonds, he thinks he can repay Nick by letting him in on the action. Nick quickly turns him down. In the novel, he explains his decision: "Because the offer was obviously and tactlessly for a service to be rendered, I had no choice except to cut him off there."[1] The emphasis is on Nick's integrity and Gatsby's coarseness. In the film, the emphasis is on Gatsby's confusion, his inability to understand that anyone would do anyone else a favor without expecting something in return,. "'A favor?'" Gatsby asks, and the screenplay elaborates on his question with this direction: "as if no one has ever done him a favor before."[2]

If readers feel a rising taste of bile, as I sometimes do, when reading *The Great Gatsby*, it may be because with one or two exceptions, mostly involving Nick, no one in the novel does anyone any favors. Or, if they do, they expect something in return. At best, the relationships that characters form with one another are transactional. At worst, they are exploitative. That goes for the many servants depicted in the novel, which may not surprise us, but also for those who do not serve, or those who resist thinking of themselves as servants. In *The Great Gatsby*, a culture of wealth corrupts connections between human beings. A novel obsessed with servants— butlers, chauffeurs, maids—turns into a novel in which all relationships turn servile. Such relationships reduce others into objects to be used and then discarded, sent to the infamous ash heaps with the husks of other exploited resources. From this perspective, what is striking about *The Great*

Gatsby is not thwarted love or the illusion of the American Dream but how few friends the characters have in the novel, how lonely the novel can seem. Before we judge the isolated world Fitzgerald creates, however, we ought to take a look at our own.

I

Recall that Nick rejects Gatsby when the latter, out of gratitude, offers to include the former in his bond scheme. The reason is that "the offer was obviously and tactlessly for a service to be rendered." Nick is insulted to think that his favor would be interpreted as a service. He objects, that is, to being mistaken for a servant, someone who performs a service in the expectation of a return. Doing so would make him no better than a butler, a chauffeur, a maid, or even the police commissioner for whom Gatsby does a favor and who in return sends him a Christmas card that lets Gatsby speed with impunity.

Nick has good reasons to refuse the association. Servants in *The Great Gatsby* perform many functions, few of them ennobling. As I described in chapter 1, Thorstein Veblen outlines two modes of demonstrating wealth: conspicuous consumption and conspicuous leisure. Perhaps because today the wealthiest of the American wealthy work for a living—as operators of hedge funds, as owners of corporations—and pride themselves on how hard they work, conspicuous consumption now matters more to our notion of wealth than conspicuous leisure does.[3] Even so, conspicuous leisure remains a viable mode of demonstrating wealth.

For conspicuous leisure, the wealthy must demonstrate they can waste not only money, which would fall under the heading of conspicuous consumption, but time. "The pervading principle and abiding test of good breeding," Veblen observes, "is the requirement of a substantial and patent waste of time."[4] That means devoting their lives to pursuits that produce nothing of any real value. Here again one might think of Tom Buchanan and his polo ponies. Or Dan Cody, the man who adopts Gatsby and gives him his first taste of wealth. Gatsby joins him on his yacht while Cody is sailed around the continent three times for, it seems, no good reason at all. With Cody as a model, Gatsby intuits the rules of the conspicuous lesiure game. He learns to fly a hydroplane, who knows why, and offers to take Nick up in it. And when he gives Nick an account of his life, he informs him that after his parents died and he inherited wealth, he "'lived like a young rajah in all the capitals of Europe—Paris, Venice, Rome—collecting jewels, chiefly rubies, hunting big game, painting a little, things for myself only.' "[5] Gatsby has invented all of it, but he knows that if he confessed the truth about how he worked and continues to work for his wealth, others would, as Tom and Daisy eventually do, think the less of him. "Well, he certainly must have strained himself to get this menagerie together," Tom comments of the Gatsby mansion and parties.[6] The sin here is to have strained.

The truly wealthy, however, can flaunt their idleness not just by wasting their own time but by purchasing and wasting the time of others. In the past and, to a certain extent, even today, wealthy men can start by exempting their wives from labor. Indeed, Daisy Buchanan has so little to do that she is reduced to wondering, "'What'll we do with ourselves this afternoon . . . and the day after that, and the next thirty years?'"[7] For the wealthy, mistresses, especially kept women, serve a similar purpose as women who can be free from productive labor. Consider Myrtle, who goes from pumping gas in Queens to buying dresses and throwing parties in Manhattan in the apartment Tom rents for her.

But wealthy men can only have so many wives—and mistresses—at a time, so they must look elsewhere for time to waste. Hence the value of servants. Servants, usually women, can be hired to complete tasks—cooking, cleaning, raising children—that used to fall to wives. Daisy's daughter appears just once in the novel—in the care of a nurse. But if the wealthy truly want to distinguish themselves, they can purchase and waste the time of men. By this logic, the stronger and more powerful the man the better. If you want to impress others by demonstrating how much time and productive energy you can waste, it pays to purchase and waste the time and energy of those who could otherwise produce the most.[8]

In life, servants must be conspicuous to demonstrate the wealth of their employers. They may be ignored, but they need to be seen. In the life of a novel, however, servants can be conspicuous or inconspicuous.[9] In *The Great Gatsby*, they come and go like fireflies at dusk, often invisible but occasionally flashing into life.

In the first chapter of *Gatsby*, servants are conspicuous mostly for their absence or, better said, their ghostly presence. Jordan refuses, but Tom accepts one of "the four cocktails just in from the pantry," as though the cocktails strolled in themselves.[10] Later, at a Gatsby party, the drinks will perform another levitating act: "The bar," Nick observes, "is in full swing, and floating rounds of cocktails permeate the garden outside."[11] And a few pages after that, when Nick is at the party with Jordan, "a tray of cocktails floated at us through the twilight."[12]

When servants do appear, they often figure as the butt of a joke. Early in the novel, after Tom, Daisy, Jordan, and Nick sit down to dinner, the butler keeps interrupting the already awkward occasion to summon Tom to speak with his mistress, Myrtle, on the phone. While he is gone, Daisy lets Nick in on what she calls "a family secret." "It's about the butler's nose," she teases. "Do you want to hear about the butler's nose?" "That's why I came over tonight," Nick cleverly responds. Daisy tells a story, who knows how accurate, about the butler and his previous job as a silver polisher for a wealthy family. It began to affect his nose, she says. "Things went from bad to worse," Jordan adds. "Yes, things went from bad to worse," Daisy confirms, observing, callously, that "finally [the butler] had to give up his position."[13]

In the fifth chapter, after Nick has excused himself so

Gatsby and Daisy can reunite, Nick observes a maid opening the upstairs windows of Gatsby's mansion. Leaning out from one of them, she "spat meditatively into the garden."[14] Curiously, it is her spitting that leads Nick to conclude that it is time he went back to Gatsby and Daisy. By arranging Gatsby and Daisy's reunion, perhaps he fears he has become more like the maid than a man.

So it goes in *The Great Gatsby*. Servants are less people than punchlines. No wonder, then, that characters like Nick, though he is not alone, do all they can to avoid the taint of service. Alas, that does not prevent them from serving, for service is not limited to uniformed servants. Each of the characters in the novel uses someone else or is used by someone else, even if no money changes hands. (Although often enough it does.) And here the novel begins to affect my nose. Here is a cross section:

1. As a young soldier stationed in Louisville, Gatsby uses Daisy ("takes her") before eventually falling in love with her.
2. Although she will later claim to have loved Tom, Daisy marries him, at least in part, for his money.
3. Fitzgerald implies that Jordan Baker, the golf champion, bribes her caddy and a witness to cover up what would have been the scandal of her cheating in a golf tournament.
4. Tom uses Myrtle for sex.
5. Myrtle uses Tom to boost her status and escape her "spiritless" husband.

6. The partygoers use Gatsby for his lavish parties.
7. Gatsby uses the partygoers to attract Daisy to his mansion.

I could go on. But let two more examples—Meyer Wolfsheim and Tom Buchanan—stand in for the rest.

At their lunch in Manhattan, Wolfsheim displays to Nick the two human molars he uses for cufflinks, which, if it means anything at all, means he literally uses another body for his own macabre sense of fashion. After their lunch, Gatsby casually tells Nick that Wolfsheim is the man who fixed the 1919 World Series. In other words, Wolfsheim has profited by turning an entire team of baseball players—eight of them, anyway—into his paid servants. That is simply how Wolfsheim relates to people. He uses them. After Gatsby is killed, Nick visits Wolfsheim and asks if he started Gatsby in business. "Start him? I made him," Wolfsheim says. When "he told me he was an [Oxford man] I knew I could use him good," he adds. Use him he does. "Right off," Wolfsheim says mysteriously, "he did some work for a client of mine up to Albany."[15]

His only rival in exploiting others may be Tom, who uses just about everyone: Daisy, Myrtle, and worst of all, George Wilson. On the way to Manhattan, Tom, with Nick and Jordan along for the ride, drives the garish yellow car that belongs to Gatsby. Tom stops for gas and once again teases Wilson about selling him a car. On the way back from Manhattan, after Tom has forced Daisy to renounce Gatsby,

Daisy is driving the yellow car with Gatsby riding shotgun. It is she who runs over Myrtle. On his way back, Tom stops at the scene of the wreck and pulls aside a shocked Wilson to insist that the yellow car he was driving earlier did not belong to him.

When Wilson goes on the hunt for the person who killed his wife, he starts, naturally enough, by asking Tom whom the yellow car does belong to. At this point, Tom hangs a target on Gatsby. He tells Wilson that Gatsby owns the car. Wilson proceeds to Gatsby's mansion and murders him. In other words, Tom uses Wilson to eliminate a rival for his wife. He gets away with it, too, not least by bribing, or so Fitzgerald implies, Myrtle's sister, Catherine, to cover up his connection to Myrtle.

One of the few genuinely intimate moments in the novel is all the more horrifying because of its intimacy. After Daisy has killed Myrtle and forsaken Gatsby, Nick watches Tom and her sitting at their kitchen table. Tom is talking and "in his earnestness his hand had fallen upon and covered her own." "There was an unmistakable air of natural intimacy about the picture," Nick observes, "and anybody would have said that they were conspiring together."[16] The family that conspires together stays together, especially if they conspire to escape the consequences of manslaughter.

Notice that Nick is not on my list of those who use others. True, Nick has hired the woman whom he calls the "demo-niac Finn" to make his bed, cook his breakfast, and mutter

"Finnish wisdom to herself."[17] But compared to the rest of the characters in the novel, he is a saint. He is, as he tells Tom in the beginning of the novel, "a bond man."[18] He means what he does for a living but also how he lives. Unlike most if not all of the characters in the book, he uses no one. He commits, with no expectation of a return, to the bonds he makes with others. Fittingly, he works at Probity Trust. Thus Gatsby is wrong about Nick. He is not selling bonds—not the figurative ones anyway. He is keeping them. For Gatsby, however, and for the rest of the characters in the novel, bonds are saleable items. You are either a bond man, like Nick, or you trade or sell bonds, like virtually everyone else.

Perhaps that is why Gatsby has such fond memories of Dan Cody, who, like Wolfsheim, gives him his start. Asked about a picture of him that Gatsby keeps in his bedroom, Gatsby sweetly refers to him as his "best friend."[19] That his best friend has been dead for over a decade, and he has made no new one in between, is telling.

It should not surprise us—though it should disturb us—that when Gatsby dies, virtually no one comes to his funeral, despite Nick trying to recruit anyone he can. Here the language of bonds returns. After Gatsby is shot, Nick is "surprised and confused" to realize that he is now responsible for Gatsby.[20] Staring at Gatsby's corpse, Nick imagines Gatsby begging him to find someone for him and pleading that he "can't go through this alone."[21] Yet Gatsby does go through it alone. As Nick puts it, "No one else was interested—interested, I mean, with that intense personal interest to which everyone has some vague right at the end."[22] The pun here is on the word *interest*, which, in the context Nick uses it, means a concern for or a devotion to something or, in this case, someone. In the language of bonds, however, interest means the rate charged for borrowed money. With the possible, fleeting exception of Daisy, the bonds others form with Gatsby are about financial interest, about the profit and loss. Nick appeals to Gatsby's supposedly "closest friend," Wolfsheim, who tells Nick he cannot get mixed up in the funeral for his friend and protégé.[23] The partygoer Nick calls Owl-Eyes does show up at the funeral and, shocked by the poor turnout, observes that people came to Gatsby parties "by the hundreds." Yet none have shown up for his funeral. He then utters a fitting epitaph for Gatsby: "The poor son-of-a-bitch."[24] Except for Nick, Owl-Eyes, and his estranged father, the only people who show up to the funeral are servants. For Gatsby, the world has turned upside down. The servants feel more of a connection to him than anyone else. Only Nick feels "a scornful solidarity" with Gatsby.[25] Not even Daisy sends "a message or a flower."[26]

Nick travels East to learn the bond business. By the end of the novel, he has learned more about bonds, financial and personal, than he would like, enough to turn his stomach and send him back to Minnesota.

II

One hundred years later, what is the state of our bonds with other people? Such a question is impossible to answer, but we can speak generally. Like graphs that show the percentage of wealth claimed by the top 1 percent, the number of servants in the United States follows a U-shaped pattern, peaking in 1930, bottoming out in the years between 1940 and 1980, and then launching upward again. That pattern should not surprise us, for the wealthy attract servants like flies to garbage, and the United States has been turning out the wealthy at heretofore unseen rates. Between 2000 and 2020, the number of billionaires in the United States, adjusting for inflation, increased from 243 to 735.[27] And the number of high, very high, and ultra-high-net-worth individuals increased even more rapidly.[28] Those people do not polish their own silver or take care of their own children.

Does an increase in the number of servants correspond with a deterioration of our other relationships? Does the commodification of people trickle down? Here too we cannot know whether the bonds we form with others have become more transactional, but we can know what has happened with the number of friends we do or do not have and how lonely we have become. In 2021, the Survey Center on American Life compared the state of friendships now with their state in the recent past. In 1990, only 3 percent of Americans reported having no close friends. In 2021, 12 percent did. In 1990, 33 percent of Americans reported having ten close friends or more. In 2021? Just 13 percent.[29] Nor is the declining number of friends a matter of choice. As the number of friends a person has declines, so does their dissatisfaction with the number of friends they have.

The Survey Center on American Life offers a couple of reasons for why friendship has declined so much. The Covid-19 pandemic, when the survey occurred, obviously affected friendships. But the pandemic does not explain all or even most of the decline. Rather, the authors of the study point to "broader structural forces" responsible for what the historian Anton Jäger calls the "friendship recession."[30] Americans marry later and move more often. Parents today devote twice as much time to their children as their parents did, which limits their chances to make and spend time with friends. And Americans work and travel for work more than ever before.

The advent of online life has not saved us from friendlessness either. If anything, it has made it worse. Staying home, as the journalist Matthew Yglesias has put it, "has become a lot less boring" than it was in the past.[31] Instead of going out with friends or going out to make them, many Americans sit in front of their screens interacting with virtual friends, who in all but a very few instances do not count as real friends.

As in *The Great Gatsby*, our friendlessness does not bode well. The Harvard Study of Adult Development, begun in 1938, followed generations of men from vastly different social backgrounds, both Harvard sophomores and boys from Boston's poorest neighborhoods. (The study eventually expanded to include their wives and children.) The study finds that how satisfied a person is with their relationships at age fifty best predicted their happiness, physical health, and mental health at age eighty. As the current director of the study, Robert Waldinger, starkly puts it, "Loneliness kills." It is, he adds, "as powerful as smoking or alcoholism." Worse, "at any given time more than one in five Americans will report that they're lonely." [32]

Indeed, loneliness is having its moment. Making Caring Common, a program of the Harvard Graduate School of Education, recently released a report, "Loneliness in America," that paints an even more dire picture. It defines loneliness as "the negative feelings that emerge from a perceived gap between one's desired and actual relationships." By that definition, 36 percent of "respondents reported feeling lonely 'frequently' or 'almost all of the time.'" [33] Even the Surgeon General has joined the chorus of those bewailing loneliness. In a 2023 op-ed for the *New York Times*, Vivek H. Murphy described his own bout with loneliness and how far loneliness had infiltrated American life. [34] In life-threateningly dull prose, the Surgeon General's Advisory on "Our Epidemic of Loneliness and Isolation" calculates that about one in two adults report feeling lonely. [35]

At first, it may seem implausible to blame a culture of wealth for the deterioration and disappearance of friendship. But it may not be so far-fetched. Over the last fifty years, neoliberalism, hyper-capitalism, laissez-faire—call it what you like—has created a massive amount of wealth for a small slice of the population. It has also affected the lives of those who did not share in that wealth. The higher stakes of who graduates from college and who does not is one reason, probably the most important, for why parents from middle- and upper-middle-class families devote so much time to their children, even as they have fewer of them. A child left to themselves is a child destined for poverty, or so the thinking goes. Our version of capitalism also requires many people to work two or more jobs, leaving next to no time to develop and maintain friendships outside of work.

Hyper-capitalism has also undermined the institutions and infrastructure that once enabled people to connect with others, to bowl in leagues rather than alone, as Robert Putnam in his book *Bowling Alone* might put it. The deindustrialization of the 1980s and 1990s did not just destroy the livelihoods of workers but also their opportunities for forming and sustaining friendships. Much the same could be said for the decline of unions. In the 1930s and well into the twentieth century, the International Ladies' Garment Workers' Union and the United Auto Workers did not only bargain for workers in the union, thereby creating more leisure time for them, but provided those workers with a whole world of sociality. The Educational Department of the ILGWU offered classes in economics, music appreciation, current events, athletics, dancing, and, unlikeliest of all, Esperanto. Tens of thousands of workers took the classes. The UAW organized softball leagues.[36]

Is there a solution to this friendship recession? A cure for the epidemic of loneliness? The reports from Harvard and the Surgeon General do not offer much hope. The Harvard Study starts on the right foot by seeking to "normalize" loneliness, much as we previously normalized depression, and to increase awareness of some of its causes, namely, "self-defeating mind-sets and behaviors." The Harvard Study also calls for a renewal of teaching people, especially children, that how we treat others should matter as much or more than our achievements or our happiness. At the moment, we have the commitments backwards. But things go downhill from there, bottoming out with the resolve that workplaces "should intentionally create community." Ignore for the moment that more and more people work from home. Short of a company picnic, how is a landscaping company going to intentionally create community?

Instead of offering one or two solutions to the epidemic of loneliness, the Surgeon General lists so many institutions and practices in need of reform that readers—at least this one—leave feeling overwhelmed and certain that none of the reforms will ever happen. More hopefully, Stephanie Cacioppo, one of the leading scientists of loneliness, developed a pill—I am not making this up—that alleviated the symptoms of loneliness and, in doing so, helped the lonely connect with others. She soon abandoned the effort, however, out of fear for its side effects and the possibility that non-pharmaceutical options might produce similar outcomes. She now promotes the acronym GRACE: "Gratitude, Reciprocity, Altruism, Choice, and Enjoyment."[37]

Unfortunately, these virtues cannot undo the structural developments—deindustrialization, fear of falling out of the professional-managerial class, so-called social media—that have led to a crisis of friendship and an epidemic of loneliness. Sophisticated Marxists prefer to distance themselves from the base-superstructure model that posits capitalism as the source for all of the other formations and practices in a given society. However vulgar, that model nevertheless describes loneliness and the crisis of friendship quite well. Save for a radical change in capitalism or putting the genie of social media back in the bottle, which would also require a radical change in capitalism, our efforts to invigorate friendship and community will reach their limits rather quickly. More to the point, the efforts will start and stop with what individuals can do to revive their friendships and their participation in community. Yet loneliness, ironically, is a social problem. In addition to individual reforms, we would need to create the economic conditions—higher wages, fewer hours, less fear about what will happen if children do not go to college—that would enable people to only connect, as the novelist E. M. Forster puts it in *Howards End*.

As it does in so many other respects, *The Great Gatsby* offers a warning. It illustrates what happens when our relationships become transactional, become this for that, so much so that the novel begins to feel dystopian. It also illustrates that such relationships are fragile, easily broken—and easily betrayed.

Now, when I think of the novel, I often think of the figure of Gatsby, surveying one of his parties, "standing alone on the marble steps."[38] Like Gatsby, too many of us stand alone.

CHAPTER FOUR

"We're All White Here"

You're one of that bunch that hangs around with Meyer Wolfsheim.

—TOM BUCHANAN TO GATSBY

A specter haunts *The Great Gatsby*: racism. The novel has three or four scenes that will disgust contemporary readers, including a reader like me who has a charitable attitude toward the novel.

As but one example, and by no means the worst, consider how the novel depicts immigrants, probably from Italy or Greece, as Nick and Gatsby drive in Gatsby's bright yellow car over the Queensborough Bridge to Manhattan:

A dead man passed us in a hearse heaped with blooms, followed by two carriages with drawn blinds and by more cheerful carriages for friends. The friends looked out at us with the tragic eyes and short upper lips of south-eastern Europe, and I was glad that the sight of Gatsby's splendid car was included in their somber holiday.[1]

The problem here is stereotyping, the assumption that everyone from "south-eastern Europe" shares one or more characteristics, in this case tragic eyes and short upper lips. I have no idea—and have not been able to discover—why everyone from south-eastern Europe supposedly had tragic eyes and short upper lips. I could not even say what short upper lips or tragic eyes look like or what, besides this funeral procession, their bearers have to feel tragic about. (Maybe because everyone believes they have tragic eyes and short upper lips?) Regardless, in this scene Nick distinguishes between us (Nick, Gatsby, their non-tragic eyes, their well-proportioned lips) and them. That distinction matters because just as 2025 marked the centenary of *The Great Gatsby*, 2024 marked the centenary of the Johnson-Reed Act—better known as the Immigration Act—of 1924. That piece of legislation sought to dam the flow of immigrants from Southern and Eastern Europe, which had turned many Americans into anxious and angry nativists.

This book, *A Rotten Crowd*, is about wealth and how it has distorted public and private life in the United States over the last fifty years. It is not, ostensibly, a book about race. In this chapter, however, I argue that wealth and race belong to the same conversation. I also turn from championing *The Great Gatsby* and what it can tell readers about wealth, to diagnosing the novel, pointing out ways that Fitzgerald—and his creation, Nick—let their prejudices get in the way of a more politically hopeful critique of wealth.

By the end of the novel, Nick has no side to take except his own, and so he retreats from riotous and diverse New York City to his birth city, the calmer, whiter, and middle-class world of St. Paul, Minnesota. His situation foreshadows the predicament many whites face today. By no means rich, they nevertheless distinguish themselves from people of color. This misplacement of loyalties may leave them feeling racially richer, but it does not leave them economically better off. Nor does it leave the poor, the working class, and people of color better off.

I

Before proceeding any further, it pays to keep in mind one way of thinking about stereotyping in the novel. That approach would distinguish between Fitzgerald the author and Nick the character. It would insist that Fitzgerald is not necessarily Nick, and Nick is not necessarily Fitzgerald. In the above passage, for example, Fitzgerald invents the funeral procession that passes Gatsby and Nick on its way to Manhattan. He may also invent how Nick responds to that scene. By that light, Fitzgerald the man may not think those from south eastern Europe have tragic eyes and short upper lips. Rather, he may stage the encounter so readers can understand the kind of person Nick is. In other words, Fitzgerald has no such prejudices, but he sets up Nick to reveal his. In which case, Fitzgerald may cast Nick as a not entirely reliable (nor entirely faultless) narrator.

Unfortunately, at least for those who want to save Fitzgerald from some of the uglier passages in the novel, that approach does not always pass the eye test, not least because in his letters and other novels, Fitzgerald occasionally shared some of the same prejudices toward ethnic and racial minorities that Nick does. In *The Great Gatsby* in particular, the distance between Fitzgerald and Nick often blurs.[2]

Consider how Nick—and Fitzgerald—handle the character of Meyer Wolfsheim. Nick first encounters Wolfsheim when he meets Gatsby for lunch in Manhattan. Here is how Nick describes him: "A small, flat-nosed Jew raised his large head and regarded me with two fine growths of hair which luxuriated in either nostril. After a moment I discovered his tiny eyes in the half darkness." Here too you could say that Fitzgerald stays in the background, creates the character of Meyer Wolfsheim, and invites readers to judge Nick for trading in anti-Semitic tropes. In other words, you could argue that Nick, as he does during the encounter on the bridge, picks out and comments on the most stereotypical features of Wolfsheim. Indeed, Nick remarks several times on his "expressive" or "tragic" nose.

But that reading seems doubtful. For the plot of the novel

to work, Fitzgerald needs someone to play the role Wolfsheim does of criminal, manipulator, and fair-weather friend. (On the last item, see the previous chapter on bonds.) That character, however, does not need to be Jewish. Nor does he need, in a nod to Shylock and his pound of flesh, to have human molars for cufflinks. Nor does he need to show off his cufflinks to Nick before Nick has even noticed them. Nor does he need to have fixed and profited from that most American of pastimes, the World Series. Nor does the villain need to be named "Wolfsheim," which clumsily appends a rapacious animal to a Jewish surname. These characterizations exist independently of how Nick perceives them. Instead, Fitzgerald retails stereotypes of Jewish people that he thinks readers will recognize and share.[3]

Still, many of the uglier moments in the novel *do* belong to its characters and not necessarily to Fitzgerald. Or, better said, Fitzgerald leaves some room between him and his characters. Take Tom. In the opening pages of the first chapter, when Nick, Tom, Jordan, and Daisy sit down to dinner, Tom seizes on Nick's innocuous remark to Daisy that she "make[s] him feel uncivilized" to launch into a diatribe on race. The whole passage, which Nick narrates, is worth quoting:

> "Civilization's going to pieces," broke out Tom violently. "I've gotten to be a terrible pessimist about things. Have you read 'The Rise of the Colored Empires' by this man Goddard?"

85

"Why, no," I answered, rather surprised by his tone.

"Well, it's a fine book, and everybody ought to read it. The idea is if we don't look out the white race will be—will be utterly submerged. It's all scientific stuff; it's been proved."

"Tom's getting very profound," said Daisy, with an expression of unthoughtful sadness. "He reads deep books with long words in them. What was that word we—"

"Well, these books are all scientific," insisted Tom, glancing at her impatiently. "This fellow has worked out the whole thing. It's up to us, who are the dominant race, to watch out or these other races will have control of things."

"We've got to beat them down," whispered Daisy, winking ferociously toward the fervent sun.

"You ought to live in California—" began Miss Baker, but Tom interrupted her by shifting heavily in his chair.

"This idea is that we're Nordics. I am, and you are, and you are, and—" After an infinitesimal hesitation, he included Daisy with a slight nod, and she winked at me again. "—And we've produced all the things that go to make a civilization— oh, science and art, all that. Do you see?"

There was something pathetic in his concentration as if his complacency, more acute than of old, was not enough to him anymore.[4]

For reasons of his own, Fitzgerald has changed the actual author and title of the book to which Tom refers. It is not *The Rise of the Colored Empires* by Goddard but *The Rising Tide of Color: The Threat Against White World Supremacy* (1920) by Lothrop Stoddard (Figure 4.1). (No genius, Tom could also just mix things up. Another eugenicist, Henry Goddard, published an influential work in 1912.)[5] The original title survives, however, when Tom insists that the white race will be "submerged." Tides submerge, empires conquer. In any case, Tom has grasped the essentials.

Stoddard divided the world into five "primary races" and their geographic homes: yellow (Asia), brown (the Middle East), black (Africa), red (Central and South America), and white (Europe and North America). Outnumbering the white race, the rest of the races threaten white supremacy and, as Tom Buchanan puts it, "all the things that go to make a civilization," which the white race and the white race alone created. But white supremacy also faces a threat from within. Stoddard divided the white race into three "sub-species—the Nordics, the Alpines, and the Mediterraneans."[6] Of these, Nordics formed "the Great Race."[7] In the United States, the greatest threat to Nordics came from the Alpines, those from Central and Eastern Europe, and the Mediterraneans, those from "south-eastern Europe," especially Italy. In a 1924 book, *Racial Realities in Europe*, Stoddard summarized his earlier thesis: "In the United States especially, recent immigration has brought in floods of Alpine and Mediterranean blood, and unless immigration from Southern and Eastern Europe is restricted and kept restricted the racial character of the American people will be rapidly and radically altered."[8] Altered for the worse, it goes without saying.

Far from a marginal figure, Stoddard and his theories had an enormous influence in America. The *New York Times* reviewed and recommended *The Rising Tide of Color*. Then Vice President Calvin Coolidge repackaged the ideas in a 1921 article for *Good Housekeeping* with the incendiary title "Whose Country Is This?" Elected president in 1924, Coolidge would make good on the Stoddard hope for "restricted" immigration by signing the 1924 Immigration Act. Stoddard also shared a publisher (Scribner's) and a medium (*The Saturday Evening Post*) with Fitzgerald.

The Rising Tide of Color explains some of the mysteries in the dinner scene. When Jordan says Tom "ought to live in California," she does not mean that Tom could escape the rise of the colored empires by fleeing to that state. She means that if Tom thinks the East has it bad, he should see California. According to Stoddard, that state shows what happens when the colored empire unseats white supremacy. Stoddard viewed California as an all but lost cause, overwhelmed by Chinese laborers imported by "unscrupulous business interests."[9]

Critics have also wondered—or glossed over—why Tom hesitates to include Daisy on his roster of Nordics. Fay—as in Daisy Fay, her maiden name—is an Irish surname, and Stoddard never says one way or the other whether the Irish count as Nordic.[10] By hesitating to include Daisy, Tom

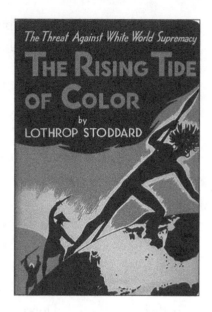

Figure 4.1. The astonishingly racist cover of Stoddard's *The Rising Tide of Color*. In order, the Black, Yellow, and Brown races bestride the globe.

resurrects an uncertainty about what race the Irish belonged to, an uncertainty captured in the title of the 1995 book by the historian Noel Ignatiev, *How the Irish Became White*. (The short answer is by hating Blacks.) That may be why Daisy ironically insists, "We've got to beat them down," and why she winks "ferociously toward the fervent sun." Daisy does not believe we need to beat them down, least of all if Tom suspects she may not belong to the "we" but to the "them." (Born to Irish parents, Fitzgerald may wink here as well.)

Interesting as they are, these details may matter less than the overall purpose of the passage, which is to cast Tom as a racist blowhard.[11] Here, Fitzgerald summons readers to join Daisy in ironically labeling Tom "very profound" and to follow Nick in thinking him "pathetic." Later in the chapter, Nick will observe that "Something was making [Tom] nibble at the edge of stale ideas."

Yet the dinner scene makes a later one, easily the most racist passage in the book, incredibly strange, for it implicates Nick in also nibbling at the edge of stale racist ideas. Just after the funeral procession of south-eastern Europeans passes Gatsby and Nick on the Queensborough Bridge, they are overtaken by another car:

> As we crossed Blackwell's Island a limousine passed us, driven by a white chauffeur, in which sat three modish negroes, two bucks and a girl. I laughed aloud as the yolks of their eyeballs rolled toward us in haughty rivalry.
>
> "Anything can happen now that we've slid over this bridge," I thought, "anything at all."
>
> Even Gatsby could happen, without any particular wonder.[12]

"Modish"—that is, fashionable—implies that the passengers in the car are following trends and in doing so have risen above their station. So too, of course, does their overturning of the customary hierarchy in which Blacks serve Whites. (The chauffeur is white.) The "negroes" in this passage may have transcended their status, but for Nick they have not transcended their race. No matter their wealth, Nick still refers to the two men as "bucks" and still sees, when he looks at them, features—"the yolks of their eyeballs"—that connect them to some of the foundational stereotypes of African Americans. (What is it with Nick and eyes?) As Nick sees them, the two men recall the minstrel character Zip Coon, the urban dandy who, in trying to imitate fashionable whites, unintentionally makes a fool of himself.

All the same, Nick supplements his racism with a not unwelcome sense of possibility. True, he laughs aloud at the "modish negroes" impersonating their betters. But to him they also represent something radical and not altogether unwelcome. In the passage above, Gatsby is included in the category of radical possibilities that could happen. He is thus connected, indirectly, with the modish negroes. As I discuss in chapter 1 on clothes, he too wears "modish" clothes. In transforming himself from James Gatz into Jay Gatsby, he too rises above his station. And he too, as we will see, threatens the white supremacy that Tom clings to.

Elsewhere, Nick makes the connection between Gatsby and outsiders even more directly. At a Gatsby party, Nick and Jordan speculate about where Gatsby has come from and how he got where he is. Jordan reveals that Gatsby once told her he went to Oxford, but she doesn't believe him. That leaves Nick to his own speculations. "I would have accepted without question the information that Gatsby sprang from the swamps of Louisiana or from the lower East Side of New York," he thinks. "That was comprehensible. But young men didn't—at least in my provincial inexperience I believed they didn't—drift coolly out of nowhere and buy a palace on Long Island Sound."[13]

In the 1920s, the swamps of Louisiana were home to Cajuns, the descendants of French Canadians exiled from Canada during the French and Indian War, and more to the point, Creoles, the offspring of European colonists (mostly French and Spanish) and freed slaves. And the Lower East Side, of course, was home to waves of immigrants, first German and then, when Fitzgerald writes his novel, Italian and Jewish communities, among others.

At first glance, Nick separates Gatsby from these minority races and ethnicities. Gatsby is not from those places; he is from "nowhere." Yet Gatsby is often linked with the same racial and ethnic minorities from which Nick initially distances him. (One critic has called Gatsby "off-white.")[14] At the Plaza Hotel, where Gatsby and Daisy go to announce their love, Tom associates Gatsby with those who would endanger white supremacy: "'Nowadays people begin by sneering at family life and family institutions,'" Tom blusters, "'and next they'll throw everything overboard and have intermarriage between black and white.'" It falls to Jordan to murmur, "'We're all white here.'"[15] For Tom to think the next-to-last barrier of civilization is family life and family institutions is rich since he leaves a trail of injured and dead paramours behind him. These include a chambermaid with a broken arm; whatever "little spree" happened in Chicago; and, soon enough, Myrtle. Tom equates civilization with whatever he values, in this case whiteness and old (or at least inherited) money. Tom then rides the slippery slope to believing that any threat to his values or interests must come from colored empires, broadly defined to include racial and ethnic minorities. It also includes the newly rich like Gatsby. For Tom, however, Gatsby is not just newly rich but also not quite all white. Trying to save his marriage by warning Daisy to whom she would be attaching herself, Tom exposes Gatsby as a bootlegger—and worse. He accuses Gatsby of being "'one of that bunch that hangs around with Meyer Wolfsheim.'" In other words, he maligns Gatsby through a kind of minority by association, just as earlier in the novel Nick indirectly associates him with Creoles and immigrants, including Jews like Wolfsheim, from the Lower East Side. Tom also accuses Gatsby of rising above his station, just as earlier the Blacks in the chauffeured car had risen above theirs. "'I'll be damned,'" he tells Gatsby, "'if I see how you got within a mile of [Daisy] unless you brought the groceries to the back door.'"[16]

For Tom, threats to whiteness come from the lower races and the lower classes. And for him, Gatsby counts as both.

II

So where does Nick fall in all of this? Where do his loyalties lie? Eventually with Gatsby, but after Gatsby is murdered, with no one at all. And that is the problem. Of course, Nick has his doubts about Gatsby all along. Early in the book, after the events of the novel have taken place, Nick observes that Gatsby "represented everything for which I have an unaffected scorn." He asserts that he "disapproved of him from beginning to end." But both of those declarations exaggerate. In the climactic scene at the Plaza Hotel, Nick roots for Gatsby in his standoff with Tom. Later, Nick comforts Gatsby by telling him that Tom and Daisy form "a rotten crowd" and that he is "worth the whole damn bunch put together." And after declaring that Gatsby represents everything for which he has an unaffected scorn, Nick reluctantly admits, "No, Gatsby turned out all right in the end; it is what preyed on Gatsby, what foul dust floated in the wake of his dreams" that disgusts him and sends him back home.

The foul dust that preys on Gatsby foreshadows the dust that Myrtle will die in and the dust, in the form of George Wilson, whom Tom will all but send to murder Gatsby. Once Gatsby is buried, however, Nick is left with no one to champion. He accuses Tom and Daisy of being "careless people" who "smashed up things and creatures and then retreated back into their money or their vast carelessness." Yet Nick conducts his own sort of retreat. Instead of remaining in the East to confront the rotten crowd, the foul dust, and the predators who prey, Nick returns to the Midwest generally and St. Paul specifically, places—for him—of morality, subtle prosperity, and more to the point, pristine whiteness.[17] (Recalling previous trips from the East to the West, Nick rhapsodizes about "the real snow, our snow.") That leaves Tom and Daisy and their ilk to continue to smash up things and retreat back into their money.

The novel presents only two choices: stay in the morally compromised East or escape to the morally secure Midwest. Nick chooses the latter. But nowhere does a third choice appear: reform the morally compromised East. For that to happen, Nick would have to have someone or some group he could align with. He does not. Instead, he thinks of immigrants and Blacks in grotesque stereotypes. Nick can sympathize with Gatsby, who is merely off-white, but he cannot sympathize with the truly non-white, those who might challenge capitalism and white supremacy, or, more concisely, might challenge Tom, who represents both of those ills. In short, *The Great Gatsby* does not offer any vision for what lies, or could lie, beyond a world of wealth and whiteness. That may explain why the ending of the novel, even with its romantic language—"So we beat on, boats against the current, borne back ceaselessly into the past"—often seems a little unsatisfying. There is no future, only the compromised past.

I do not think Nick needs to join the Socialist Party and take to the ramparts, especially since after the First Red Scare of 1919 there was no Socialist Party to speak of and no ramparts to climb. Rather, the argument is that his racism prevents Nick from making common cause with immigrants and Blacks. Those prejudices limit his opportunities to do anything about the rotten crowds of wealth and whiteness. They limit immigrants and Blacks from doing anything about them as well.

III

Those racial and class divisions, so long in the making, matter even today. For progressives like me, those who enjoy curling up with National Bureau of Economic Research papers, one of the most important articles of the last three decades is "Why Doesn't the United States Have a European-Style Welfare State" by Alberto Alesina, Edward Glaeser, and Bruce Sacerdote. Published in 2001, its data has fallen behind, but its thesis is as powerful as ever.

Alesina, Glaeser, and Sacerdote ask why governments of European Union (EU) countries tax and spend so much more of their gross domestic product than the United States does. The difference is stark. The average spending in 2001 of an EU government equaled 48 percent of its GDP. For the United States, it was 36 percent. (The numbers have not moved much. In 2022, it was 50 percent for EU governments and 37 percent for the United States.)[18] Over half of that difference owes to how much each country devotes to redistribution and welfare. These programs include child tax credits, sickness and accidental injury benefits, disability benefits, and poverty relief. The United States spends 11 percent of its GDP on these; the average EU country spends 18 percent.

The question is why. Alesina, Glaeser, and Sacerdote offer a couple of possibilities. One is political. The United States strains under a two-party system, a Constitution, and a legal system that enshrine the right to property above all other rights. These limit what the government can do by way of taxation and redistribution. The other, more compelling explanation is that the United States has greater racial heterogeneity than European countries, and its minorities are disproportionately represented among the poor. Thus, as a majority of (white) Americans see it, an outsized share of welfare spending goes or would go to those of a different race.[19] "The history of American redistribution," Alesina, Glaeser, and Sacerdote write, "makes it quite clear that hostility to welfare derives in part from the fact that welfare spending in the United States goes disproportionately to minorities."[20] Or, as the economist and *New York Times* columnist Paul Krugman has more colloquially written, "Republican political strategy has been exploiting racial antagonism, getting working-class whites to despise government because it dares to help Those People, for almost half a century."[21] What Krugman does not say is that Democrats have often done the same thing. They have just been a little quieter about it than Republicans have.

In *The Great Gatsby*, how racial antagonism affects welfare spending does not matter all that much. The novel takes place before there was much of a welfare state at all, and the poor make but passing appearances. Instead, *The Great Gatsby* foreshadows why it would take the United States longer than most other countries to establish a welfare state and why that state would remain stingier than others. The novel also illustrates why a country would want a welfare state. In order to fund it, nations have to tax their citizens, especially the rich. From this perspective, welfare spending plays two roles: it helps those who need help, and it also limits runaway wealth and all the problems that runaway wealth creates. In other words, if Nick had more sympathy for immigrants from south eastern Europe and Blacks in the United States, he might create the possibility for more support to the poor writ large. More to the point, he might constrain Tom and Daisy and careless people like them from smashing "up things and retreating back into their money or their vast carelessness." Simply put, the wealthy and careless would have less money to retreat into. In stereotyping minorities, that is, Nick indirectly enables the rich.

Generations of high school and college students have read *The Great Gatsby*. Would our country look different—more attentive to the poor—if Nick had looked at the poor differently? Probably not. I do not overestimate the power of fictions. But maligning both the rich and the poor does limit what the novel can accomplish politically.

Today, when I read some of the more racist passages in *The Great Gatsby*, part of me wonders why anyone should read the book at all. Yet for all its ugliness, the novel, whether it does so intentionally or not, displays how the racism that bedeviled America in 1925 continues to bedevil it in 2025. If so, the specter that haunts *The Great Gatsby* is not racism alone, but how racism has protected and continues to protect wealth. The novel provides an origin story for where we find ourselves today, one that drags us, as in the closing lines of the book, "ceaselessly into the past" of the tragic history of whiteness.

CONCLUSION

Our Orgastic Futures

My own house was an eyesore, but it was a small eyesore, and it had been overlooked, so I had a view of the water, a partial view of my neighbor's lawn, and the consoling proximity of millionaires. . . .

—NICK CARRAWAY

Some novels begin memorably: "Call me Ishmael." "Mrs. Dalloway said she would buy the flowers herself." "Happy families are all alike; every unhappy family is unhappy in its own way." Others, like *The Great Gatsby*, save the best for last:

Gatsby believed in the green light, the orgastic future that year by year recedes before us. It eluded us then, but that's no matter—tomorrow we will run faster, stretch out our arms further. . . . And one fine morning—

Our Orgastic Futures

So we beat on, boats against the current, borne back ceaselessly into the past.[1]

The green light Gatsby believes in refers to Daisy, of course, whose dock Gatsby can see from his mansion. That is, it represents something simultaneously concrete and symbolic. Yet it also invokes something that extends beyond the confines of the novel. Call it hope. From that perspective, it does not matter what shape a green light takes, who or what it represents. Rather, what matters is that one believes in something—the green light—worth aspiring to. Those green lights do not only reside in some "orgastic future"; rather, they *are* the "orgiastic future." It has puzzled readers—and copy editors—why Fitzgerald chooses an alternate spelling of the adjective form of *orgasm*. (It is usually *orgasmic*.) My hunch is because he wants readers to understand the sexual component of what Gatsby desires—he wants Daisy—but he also wants to signal a desire for something or someone that is not necessarily sexual. The realization of that green light will be orgastic, less a sexual climax than a general one, a culmination, an apex.

Alas, that orgastic future "year by year recedes before us." We may think we can overtake it—run faster, stretch out our arms further—but we never quite catch up. We are "boats against the current," chasing the orgastic future we desire but nevertheless "borne back ceaselessly into the past." We watch, helplessly, as our green light vanishes over the horizon. The one fine morning never comes.

A Rotten Crowd

Fitzgerald leaves it to readers to define their own green light. Let me describe one of mine. The theme of this book is how the accumulation and concentration of wealth over the last fifty years has distorted American life. A culture of wealth generates heaps of disposable clothes. It wastes resources. It monetizes our relationship with others. And it maintains the divisions among races that prevent people from repairing the damage the pursuit and accumulation of wealth creates. In my green-lit orgastic future, none of this—or a lot less of it—would exist.

Now comes the time in a book like this one when readers expect writers to say how we can cure these ills. Lately, though, I have found these proposals slightly disappointing because, especially in books coming from the left side of the political spectrum, they tend to return to the same prescriptions: make it easier for workers to form and join unions; end gerrymandering; limit the role of money in political campaigns; and so on. I support all these efforts. I have recommended them in the conclusions of past books. But since we find ourselves no closer to those goals than we were twenty years ago, when I started advocating for them, and thirty years ago, when I started reading of them, maybe we should try another approach.

A lot of the problems I describe above—heaps of clothes, the waste of resources, the monetization of bonds—arise from imitation. What the wealthy buy or do influences what others buy or do. Consider houses. In 1975, the average

102

size of a newly built house was 1,660 square feet. In 2022, the average size was 2,522 square feet.[2] Keep in mind, too, that as houses have grown, the number of people in households has declined. In 1975, there were 2.94 people per household. In 2022, 2.50.[3] Thus, square footage per person has nearly doubled, from 565 in 1975 to 1,009 in 2022. Classical economists would say buyers of larger and larger houses have freely chosen what to spend their money on. People have always wanted bigger homes, economists reason, so when they have the resources to buy or build a bigger one, they do.

For the economist Robert Frank, however, the desire for a larger house—or other luxuries—does not happen in a vacuum. Rather, our expectations about what constitutes a respectable house can change. It can change because by building bigger houses, in part to outbuild each other, the wealthy influence how those below them view the world. What you and I used to consider a decent house now seems disreputably small. So, mimicking the rich, we buy bigger houses. Not as big as the wealthiest among us, but bigger nonetheless. In turn, our investment in bigger houses nudges those below us to buy bigger houses, and those below them as well, "and so on all the way down," as Frank puts it.[4] In other words, our desires are not absolute but relative.

Adam Smith, the (unlikely) hero of classical economists, recognized this phenomenon 250 years ago. "A linen shirt," he wrote in *The Wealth of Nations*, is, strictly speaking, not a necessary of life. The Greeks and Romans lived, I suppose, very comfortably though they had no linen. But in the present times, through the greater part of Europe, a creditable day-labourer would be ashamed to appear in public without a linen shirt, the want of which would be supposed to denote that disgraceful degree of poverty which, it is presumed, nobody can well fall into without extreme bad conduct.[5]

For Smith, day-laborers require some object—a sort of talisman—to distinguish themselves from the poor. In this case, a linen shirt. Those who wish to distinguish themselves from day-laborers, however, would require yet another talisman, and so on, to adapt Frank, all the way up.

Staying with the subject of shirts, Gatsby could not seem to care less about his beautiful shirts. But to distinguish himself from the poor boy who had no clothes, to compete with Tom, who has equally nice but more tasteful shirts, and to impress Daisy, Gatsby needs shirts "piled like bricks in stacks a dozen high." For Nick to impress Jordan, he too must wear nice shirts. Maybe not as nice as those Gatsby wears, but nice nonetheless. All the way down, even to George Wilson, whose wife, Myrtle, mocks him because he gets married in a borrowed suit and, presumably, an unremarkable shirt. We distinguish ourselves from each other by the shirts we wear.

One way to think about the subtle logic of distinctions is

to consider how much money Americans think a family of four needs to get by. On average, the figure is $85,000. But the average conceals a lot. As the income of respondents increases, so too does their estimate of how much money a family requires. For example, 48 percent of those who make more than $100,000 per year estimate that a family of four would need to make $100,000 or more to live comfortably. In their world, anything less than $100,000 is penury. By contrast, only 16 percent of those who make less than $40,000 per year think a family would need $100,000 or more to get by. In their world, $100,000 or more is extravagant. Starting closer to the bottom, 22 percent of those who make less than $40,000 per year think $30,000 to $50,000 would finance a decent life. Yet just 3 percent of those who make $100,000 or more believe that that income would suffice.[6] The upshot is that a majority within each class defines sufficiency by comparison with their equals or betters. As income rises, expectations of how much money it takes to live a decent life increase as well.

The lesson here is that one must keep up with the Joneses. But the Joneses vary depending on where you live and how much you and they make.

Rising inequality only worsens this dynamic. As those in the top 1 percent of households command more and more income and spend more and more of that income on houses, cars, and clothes, they make it difficult for those whose wealth has remained stagnant (basically the bottom 90 percent of Americans) to compete with their betters and with each other.

Many of them do so by going into debt. From 2004 to 2022, debt in the United States more than doubled.[7] That is great news for banks, credit card companies, and big-box stores, but less great news for those who have to pay off the debt. To adapt the quotation I borrow as my epigraph, for those without millions, the proximity of millionaires is not consoling but distressing. It also costs a fortune.

For Frank, how the wealthy spends their money functions like a contagion: "The runaway spending at the top has been a virus," he writes, "one that's spawned a luxury fever that, to one degree or another, has all of us in its grip."[8] In addition to being contagious, chasing after our betters and outcompeting our equals is also wasteful. We spend more and more money on things—larger houses, nicer cars—we do not need but that we perceive as needs because of the neighborhood and culture we live in. According to that culture, everyone needs a new—and better—car every three to five years.

The sociologist Pierre Bourdieu called this dynamic "the competitive struggle": "One class possesses a particular property, another class catches up with it," which leaves the first class at pains to distinguish itself from the class that caught up with it. And the struggle never stops. For Bourdieu, the question is not how to win this contest but how to escape it. "What is the moment," he asks, "when the probability of having one's interests satisfied by remaining in the race ceases to be greater than the possibility of having them satisfied by leaving the race?" In other words, when will people awake and realize that, as the 1983 film *War Games* had it, the only winning move is not to play? "That is how," Bourdieu believes, "the historical question of revolution arises."[9]

A few people have the independence of mind to drop out of the race. Those committed to FIRE—Financial Independence, Retire Early—may see through the competitive struggle, as may those who follow the advice in the cult book *Your Money or Your Life* by Vicki Robin and Joe Dominguez, first published in 1992 but now in its third edition. But those people are rare. Indeed, Frank thinks evolution demands that we play the game: "There is compelling evidence that concerns about relative position is a deep-rooted and ineradicable element of human nature."[10] If so, then "the problem cannot be solved at the individual level."[11]

How can it be solved? Frank supports what he calls a progressive consumption tax. Households can do one of two things with the money they earn: save it or spend it. A progressive consumption tax would not tax savings, but it would tax spending. Assume a family of four earns $100,000 and, after deductibles and savings, spends $50,000 of its income. That is the amount a progressive consumption tax would tax. A family at that income level might pay a tax rate of 10 percent on what it spends, thus a progressive consumption tax on that family would yield $10,000, or 10 percent of its income. By contrast, consider a family of four that earned one million dollars and also spent half of its income ($500,000) on goods and services. Instead of 10 percent, it might have a consumption tax rate of 50 percent. That would translate into $250,000 in taxes and an overall tax rate of 25 percent. Hence the "progressive" part of a progressive consumption tax. As income—and spending—increases, the tax rate would increase as well.

Such a tax would thus confront spending from two directions. It would encourage saving by shielding savings from taxes, and it would discourage spending by taxing spending.

A progressive consumption tax would therefore lower the luxury fever that, Frank thinks, infects us all. If it costs the wealthy to spend more money on houses, then they would spend less money on houses, and those below them would not need to spend as much of their money on houses to keep up. The wealthy could still distinguish themselves from one another and from those below them, but they would do so by building or buying slightly smaller houses. If desires are on balance relative and not absolute, then one can derive as much satisfaction from owning a house that is twice as large as the average regardless of how big the average house actually is. The same effect would obtain among those slightly less wealthy than the truly wealthy, among those slightly less wealthy than them, and among those slightly less wealthy than them. On balance, the overall price of houses would drop.[12]

Regardless of where one falls on the income ladder, spending less on houses would allow individuals to save money or to spend it on what Frank calls "categories that matter," things like shorter commute times, shorter workdays, longer vacations, and so on. Unlike larger and larger houses, which we soon take for granted and thus derive little happiness from, these types of spending are "gains that endure." (Frank calls them "inconspicuous consumption.") Equally important, whereas conspicuous consumption has, by definition, at least as many losers as winners, inconspicuous consumption is win-win. Everyone benefits from, say, shifting resources from a nicer car to a shorter workday. Investing in inconspicuous consumption has another advantage. It might rescue us from the burning through of resources that contributes to our looming environmental catastrophe. Today we focus on how alternative energy can meet existing demand. Reducing demand is even easier.

Yet a progressive consumption tax has its flaws. Not least of these is that Frank published his book in 1999, and he could not foresee the jaw-dropping concentration of wealth that would occur over the next twenty-five years. For example, in 2024 the United States had 813 billionaires. Those billionaires can make a mockery of a progressive consumption tax. Instead of spending 50 percent of their income on goods and services like those with less money, say a billionaire with an annual income of one hundred million dollars "thriftily" spends only 10 percent of those earnings—that is, ten million dollars. And say we taxed that spending at 100 percent. Their overall tax bill would be ten million dollars—or just 10 percent of their income. If you recall, that is the rate the family making $100,000 paid. There is nothing progressive about that. Even if one were to supplement a progressive consumption tax with other progressive taxes, when wealth and income soar high enough, even 100 percent consumption taxes would not inhibit spending all that much. Worse, by encouraging the wealthy to spend less and save more, a progressive consumption tax might have the unintended consequence of increasing wealth inequality. A penny saved is a penny earned. A billion pennies saved—and invested in the stock market—is God knows how many pennies earned. More than you and I can earn.

For these reasons, perhaps a progressive consumption tax is not for you. Maybe you favor a wealth tax. Or a top marginal income tax rate of 92 percent, as it was in 1953. The question is moot. Each of these proposals seems even less likely to arrive than any of the other blue-sky reforms that usually appear in the conclusions of books like this one.

So, what do we do until these reforms do come, which may be never? Here I disagree with Frank. Yes, nature may predispose us to compare ourselves to others, and yes, that may make it difficult to solve the problem of luxury fever at the individual level. But if Frank is right that inconspicuous consumption offers gains that endure, then we—not we as a culture but we as individuals—can direct as many or more of our resources to it as we do to conspicuous consumption.[13]

How so? While writing this book, I joined my local Friends Meeting, otherwise—and pejoratively—known as Quakers. I live in Pennsylvania, which William Penn originally founded as a colony where Friends, persecuted in England, could freely worship. My thinking about whether God exists did not change all that much. I may have evolved from atheist to agnostic. But I joined the Friends because they believe in virtues—equality, peace—that I share, and they offer a community of likeminded people who try to live out these virtues. For me, the most important of these "testimonies," what Friends call beliefs or commitments, is the testimony of simplicity. For the first Quakers, simplicity meant plainness in dress and in speech. Those early Quakers believed that plainness eliminated whatever might distract them from a relationship with God. In more recent years, Quakers continued to believe in eliminating superfluities, but the emphasis shifted to living without the avalanche of things Americans bury themselves under. So yes, Frank is right that a luxury fever cannot be cured at the individual level. Yet he goes too far in saying that individuals cannot escape from, as Bourdieu puts it, the competitive struggle. They can make a virtue of simplicity. As Friends demonstrate, they can and have. Unfortunately, almost everything in our culture pulls us away from that virtue. This emphasis on simplicity does not mean one surrenders the hope for a more radical solution to a culture of wealth like a progressive consumption tax, a higher top tax rate, or a plain old wealth tax. But it does offer a more meaningful and satisfying way to live in the meantime and, perhaps, for all time. Instead of or in addition to a different form of taxation, we may need a different way of life.

111

A Rotten Crowd

This thought brings us back to Gatsby. Gatsby treats Daisy as a commodity, as someone whose love must be bought. (Tom does too.) Gatsby all but says so when he declares that Daisy has a voice "full of money," or when he rhapsodically describes the upper-middle-class home of her girlhood as full of "a hint of bedrooms upstairs more beautiful and cool than other bedrooms" and "romances that were not musty…but fresh and breathing and redolent of this year's shining motor-cars."[14] And because Daisy has no other choice, she lets herself be treated as a commodity. That is where everything in the novel starts to go wrong, and the perils of commodification, and not the villainy of the wealthy, is the moral I take from the novel. Not the cliché that money can't buy you love or happiness, although that is true enough. Rather, it is that if something (or someone) requires the accumulation of wealth in order to gain it, as winning Daisy does, one ought to think hard about whether it is worth gaining at all. To think otherwise is to chase not just a green light but an *ignis fatuus*—a "false light."

Notes

Introduction: The Distressing Proximity of Millionaires

1. See https://www.nytimes.com/2008/02/17/education/17gatsby.html,
2. See https://www.nytimes.com/2013/04/26/business/media/new-great-gats-by-book-carries-a-hollywood-look.html.
3. Jed Esty, *Unseasonable Youth: Modernism, Fiction, and the Fiction of Development* (Oxford: Oxford University Press, 2012), 215.
4. See https://www.nytimes.com/2022/04/26/briefing/elon-musk-twitter-sale.html.
5. My title invokes Alan Krueger's 2012 Center for American Progress speech, "The Rise and Consequences of Inequality in the United States." In it, he argues that as inequality increases, intergenerational mobility decreases. He labels a chart illustrating the relationship, "The Great Gatsby Curve," https://obamawhitehouse.archives.gov/sites/default/files/krueger_cap_speech_final_remarks.pdf.
6. Andrew Michael Newman, "High School and The *Great Gatsby* Curve," in *The Great Gatsby*, ed. David J. Alworth (New York: W. W. Norton, 2022), 520.
7. Like a fresh college graduate with a degree in finance, Nick travels to New York to get rich, to learn "the shining secrets that only Midas and Morgan and Maecenas knew." Unlike many graduates, however, Nick ends up repelled by what he sees, by the rot that lies beneath the gold.
8. F. Scott Fitzgerald, *The Great Gatsby* (1925; New York: W. W. Norton, 2022), 27.
9. Fitzgerald, *Great Gatsby*, 99.
10. Rainier Zitelmann, *The Rich in Public Opinion: What We Think About When We Think About Wealth* (Washington, DC: Cato Institute, 2020), 49.

11. Ibid., xiv.

12. Ibid., 74. I am resisting the urge to mention that Mora served as ambassador for Francisco Franco.

13. Although there may indeed be something immoral about great wealth, that argument does not always come from the envious non-wealthy but occasionally from the wealthy themselves. In 2010, at the behest of Bill Gates and Warren Buffett, forty of the richest Americans signed on to the Giving Pledge, which binds billionaires "to publicly commit to give the majority of their wealth to philanthropy either during their lifetimes or in their wills." "About the Giving Pledge," The Giving Pledge, https://givingpledge.org/about,

14. The "may" in "may use" is generous. Among other works, see Larry Bartels, *Unequal Democracy: The Political Economy of the New Gilded Age* (Princeton: Princeton University Press, 2008).

15. Peter G. Peterson Foundation, "US Defense Spending Compared to Other Countries," https://www.pgpf.org/chart-archive/0053_defense-comparison..

16. F. Scott Fitzgerald, *A Life in Letters*, ed. Matthew J. Bruccoli (New York: Scribner's, 1995), 352.

17. True, most people entertain an image of the wealthy regardless of how much wealth they control. But how much wealth they control matters as well.

18. Fitzgerald, *Great Gatsby*, 8.

19. See F. Scott Fitzgerald, *Trimalchio: An Early Version of The Great Gatsby*, ed. James L. West III (Cambridge: Cambridge University Press, 2000); and F. Scott Fitzgerald, *The Great Gatsby: An Edition of the Manuscript*, ed. James L. West III and Don C. Skemer (Cambridge: Cambridge University Press, 2018).

20. Ibid., 78.

1. What to Wear in *The Great Gatsby*

1. "The Great Gatsby Party," https://greatgatsbyparty.com/new-york/.

2. F. Scott Fitzgerald, "What Kind of Husbands Do Jimmies' Make?," in *F. Scott Fitzgerald in His Own Time: A Miscellany*, ed. Matthew J. Bruccoli and Jackson R. Bryer (Kent, OH: Kent State University Press, 1971), 186–92.

3. Steven Benna, "25 quotes that take you inside Elon Musk's brilliant, ec-

centric mind," *Business Insider*, September 23, 2015, https://www.businessinsider.com/brilliant-elon-musk-quotes-2015-9.

4. Michael E. Porter and Nitin Nohria, "How CEOs Manage Their Time," *Harvard Business Review*, July–August 2018, https://hbr.org/2018/07/how-ceos-manage-time?&tag=petergasca.com.

5. F. Scott Fitzgerald, *The Great Gatsby* (1925; New York: W. W. Norton, 2022), 65–66.

6. Ibid., 96.

7. Ibid., 56.

8. Ibid., 61.

9. Ibid., 77.

10. Tom Buchanan may be a racist, philandering blowhard, but he is no idiot. Or not a complete idiot. When Daisy coos to Gatsby at lunch about how he always looks so cool, like the advertisement of the man, Tom realizes that his wife has fallen in love with Gatsby.

11. Fitzgerald, *Great Gatsby*, 79.

12. Ibid.

13. Ibid., 23.

14. Ibid., 24.

15. Ibid., 23.

16. Ibid., 27.

17. Ibid., 23.

18. Myrtle claims to know right away that she made a mistake marrying her husband because he gets married in a borrowed suit. When the man who loans it to him comes back for it a few days later, Myrtle lies down and cries, or so she says.

19. Fitzgerald, *Great Gatsby,* 23.

20. Pierre Bourdieu, "Haute Couture and Haute Culture," in *Sociology in Question* (London: Sage Publications, 1993), 135.

21. *The Devil Wears Prada*, directed by David Frankel, 2006, 20th Century Fox.

22. Jay Z, "Otis." Track 4 on *Watch the Throne*. Roc-A-Fella Records, Roc Nation, and Def-Jam Recordings, 2011.

23. Rachel Tashjian, "The rich don't dress like you think they do," *Washington Post*, May 7, 2023, https://www.washingtonpost.com/lifestyle/2023/05/07/quiet-luxury-succession/.

24. But these examples can exaggerate. Examine any given "Sunday Styles"

section of the *New York Times* or its *T Magazine* and the relationship among wealth, aspiration, and clothes remains as strong as ever.

25. Rachel Monroe, "Fast Fashion Is Eating the World," *Atlantic Monthly*, March 2021, https://www.theatlantic.com/magazine/archive/2021/03/ultra-fast-fashion-is-eating-the-world/617794/.

26. "Consumer Expenditures in 2018," U.S. Bureau of Labor Statistics, May 2020, https://www.bls.gov/opub/reports/consumer-expenditures/2018/home.htm.

27. Stephanie Vatz, "Why America Stopped Making Its Own Clothes," KQED, May 24, 2013, https://www.kqed.org/lowdown/7939/madein-america.

28. Bureau of Labor Statistics, "One Hundred Years of U.S. Consumer Spending," May 2006, https://www.bls.gov/opub/100-years-of-u-s-consumer-spending.pdf.

29. "Labor in the Textile and Apparel Industries," Bureau of Labor Statistics, August 1969, https://fraser.stlouisfed.org/files/docs/publications/bls/bls_1635_1969.pdf; Peter Liquori, "The History of American Made Clothing," *Goodwear*, August 30, 2017, https://www.goodwear.com/blogs/news/the-history-of-american-made-clothing; Dana Thomas, "The High Price of Fast Fashion," *Wall Street Journal*, August 19, 2019, https://www.wsj.com/articles/the-high-price-of-fast-fashion-11567096637.

30. Thomas, "The High Price of Fast Fashion."

31. Elizabeth Cline, *Overdressed: The Shockingly High Cost of Cheap Fashion* (New York: Penguin Portfolio, 2012), 43.

32. Bureau of Labor Statistics, "Fashion," June 2012, https://www.bls.gov/spotlight/2012/fashion/pdf/fashion_bls_spotlight.pdf.

33. Stephanie Clifford, "U.S. Textile Plants Return, with Floors Largely Empty of People," *New York Times*, September 19, 2013, https://www.nytimes.com/2013/09/20/business/us-textile-factories-return.html.

34. Vickie Elmer, "Finally, a Hoodie That Will Last Longer Than Your Marriage," *Quartz*, March 29, 2013, https://qz.com/68574/sustainable-fashion-for-the-mark-zuckerbergs-of-the-world-the-10-year-hoodie.

35. Nicholas Gilmore, "Ready-to-Waste: America's Clothing Crisis," *Saturday Evening Post*, January 16, 2018, https://www.saturdayeveningpost.com/2018/01/ready-waste-americas-clothing-crisis/.

36. Cline, *Overdressed*, 135.

37. Thomas, "The High Price of Fast Fashion."

38. "The *Guardian* view on fast fashion: It can't cost the earth," *The Guardian*, March 13, 2020, https://www.theguardian.com/commentisfree/2020/mar/13/the-guardian-view-on-fast-fashion-it-cant-cost-the-earth

39. Fitzgerald, *Great Gatsby*, 82.

2. Among the Ash Heaps and Millionaires

1. "Brooklyn's Plan for Ash Removal," *New York Times*, March 10, 1907, https://www.nytimes.com/1907/03/10/archives/brooklyns-plan-for-ash-removal-many-cities-to-try-system-of.html.

2. Sam Roberts, "Sports and the Wide World of Tomorrow," *New York Times*, April 27, 2005, https://www.nytimes.com/2005/04/27/nyregion/sports-and-the-wide-world-of-tomorrow.html.

3. "Brooklyn's Plan for Ash Removal."

4. "Topical Map of the counties of Kings and Queens, New York," Library of Congress, https://www.loc.gov/resource/g3804n.la000505/?r=-0.082,0.158,0.944,0.439,0.

5. Jason Munshi-South, "Development will damage Flushing Meadows' role as marshy buffer against storm surge and coastal flooding," *New York Daily News*, Dec. 3, 2012, https://www.nydailynews.com/2012/12/03/development-will-damage-flushing-meadows-role-as-marshy-buffer-against-storm-surge-and-coastal-flooding/

6. Kara Murphy Schlichting, *New York Recentered: Building the Metropolis from the Shore* (Chicago: University of Chicago Press, 2019), 198.

7. Ibid., 195.

8. F. Scott Fitzgerald, *The Great Gatsby* (1925; New York: W. W. Norton, 2022), 18.

9. Levi Asher, "In Gatsby's Tracks: Locating the Valley of Ashes in a 1924 Photo," *Literary Kicks*, February 24, 2010, https://litkicks.com/ingatsbystracks/.

10. Another allusion is to T. S. Eliot's *The Waste Land*, published in 1922, which Fitzgerald had read. Too much can be made of that reference, but the Eliot poem has a good deal of ash blanketing it as well. Gatsby also dies in his swimming pool, which is ironic since in *The Waste Land* water functions as both baptism and salvation or, in a godless world, the cruel simulacra of these.

11. "Stage 1A Archaeological Assessment," Shea Stadium Redevelopment, October 2021, 12, http://s-media.nyc.gov/agencies/lpc/arch_reports/594.pdf.
12. Fitzgerald, *Great Gatsby*, 1-2.
13. The other way to read the line, especially the word *wake*, may be as "awake." Gatsby has his dreams—mainly, recapturing Daisy. But Daisy cannot live up to his dreams. She refuses to admit she always loved him and never loved Tom, as Gatsby stubbornly demands, and in the end, she rejects Gatsby and returns to Tom, who can protect her after she has killed Myrtle. When Gatsby wakes from these dreams, it is then that the dust overtakes him, and he is preyed on and killed.
14. Fitzgerald, *Great Gatsby*, 104. Ellipses in original.
15. Ibid., 20.
16. Ibid.
17. Ibid., 27.
18. Ibid., 89.
19. Ibid., 100.
20. Ibid., 80.
21. Ibid., 95.
22. Ibid., 115.
23. Ibid., 104.
24. Ibid., 116.
25. Sclichting, *New York Recentered*, 198.
26. Robert Moses, "From Dump to Glory," *The Saturday Evening Post*, January 15, 1938, 13.
27. Ibid., 72.
28. Ibid.
29. Ibid., 12.
30. Ibid.
31. Robert Moses, "The Saga of Flushing Meadows" (New York: Triborough Bridge and Tunnel Authority, 1966), n.p., http://www.nywf64.com/saga02.shtml. The pamphlet recycles language from his 1938 *Saturday Evening Post* article.
32. Robert Moses, "Comment on a *New Yorker* Profile and Biography," August 26, 1974, 16, https://macaulay.cuny.edu/seminars/glassman08b/wp-content/uploads/2008/02/moses-response-to-power-broker.pdf.
33. By 1939, when Moses finished work on the park, Americans owned over

26 million automobiles. That amounted to nearly one car per family. If New York was not a motorized city, and if the United States were not a motorized country, they soon would be. See https://www2.census.gov/library/publications/decennial/1940/population-families/41272167ch1.pdf.

34. Approximately 27 percent. "Carbon Pollution from Transportation," U.S. Environmental Protection Agency, last updated May 11, 2023, //www.epa.gov/transportation-air-pollution-and-climate-change/carbon-pollution-transportation.

35. Jim Dwyer, "In a Flood-Troubled City, a Refreshing Argument About Climate Change," *New York Times*, November 1, 2012, https://www.nytimes.com/2012/11/02/nyregion/a-refreshing-argument-about-climate-change-and-what-to-do-about-it.html.

36. "Global Carbon Inequality," *World Inequality Report 2022*, https://wir2022.wid.world/chapter-6/.

37. Fitzgerald, *Great Gatsby*, 115.

3. "You're Selling Bonds, Aren't You, Old Sport?"

1. F. Scott Fitzgerald, *The Great Gatsby* (1925; New York: W. W. Norton, 2022), 55.

2. Baz Luhrman and Craig Pearce, *The Great Gatsby*, directed by Baz Luhrman, 2013. Warner Brothers, https://stephenfollows.com/resource-docs/scripts/greatgatsby_sp.pdf.

3. In 2016, two-thirds of those on the *Forbes* list of the 400 wealthiest Americans earned their money. One-third at least in part had inherited theirs. See https://www.chicagobooth.edu/review/never-mind-1-percent-lets-talk-about-001-percent.

4. Thorstein Veblen, *The Theory of the Leisure Class* (1899; New York: Penguin, 1994), 55.

5. Fitzgerald, *Great Gatsby*, 44.

6. Ibid., 71.

7. Ibid., 77.

8. Veblen, *Theory of the Leisure Class*, 57. Today, the more impressive show of waste would involve not strength but intelligence.

9. See Bruce Robbins, *The Servant's Hand: English Fiction from Below* (Durham, NC: Duke University Press, 1986).

10. Fitzgerald, *Great Gatsby*, 11.

11. Ibid., 29.
12. Ibid., 31.
13. Ibid., 13.
14. Ibid., 59.
15. Ibid., 110.
16. Ibid., 94.
17. Ibid., 6.
18. Ibid., 11.
19. Ibid., 62.
20. Ibid., 105.
21. Ibid., 106.
22. Ibid., 105.
23. Ibid., 110.
24. Ibid., 113.
25. Ibid., 106.
26. Ibid., 113.
27. "How Many Billionaires Are There, Anyway?," *New York Times*, April 7, 2022, https://www.nytimes.com/2022/04/07/magazine/billionaires.html.
28. Rupert Neate, "The number of global ultra-high-net-worth individuals hits record high," *The Guardian*, September 20, 2022, https://www.theguardian.com/news/2022/sep/20/number-global-ultra-high-net-worth-individuals-record-high.
29. Daniel A. Cox, "The State of American Friendship: Change, Challenges, and Loss," Survey Center of American Life, June 8, 2021, https://www.americansurveycenter.org/research/the-state-of-american-friendship-change-challenges-and-loss/. In 1990, 75 percent of Americans reported having a best friend. Now only 59 percent do, and 21 percent of people with a best friend say that it is a member of their family, usually a spouse or partner.
30. Anton Jäger, "From Bowling Alone to Posting Alone," *Jacobin*, December 5, 2022, https://jacobin.com/2022/12/from-bowling-alone-to-posting-alone.
31. Matthew Yglesias, "Sitting at home alone has become a lot less boring, and that might be bad," *Slow Boring*, August 22, 2022, https://www.slowboring.com/p/sitting-at-home-alone-has-become.
32. Liz Mineo, "Good Genes Are Nice, But Joy Is Better," *Harvard Gazette*, April 11, 2017, https://news.harvard.edu/gazette/story/2017/04/over-nearly-80-years-harvard-study-has-been-showing-how-to-live-a-healthy-

and-happy-life/. A potential problem with this argument is, of course, the tangle of correlation and causation. Does having better relationships generate healthier people? Or do healthier people have better relationships because they are healthy? Waldinger argues for the former.

33. Richard Weissbourd et al., "Loneliness in America," Making Caring Common, https://static1.squarespace.com/static/5b7c56e255b-02c683659fe43/t/6021776bdd04957c4557c212/1612805995893/Loneliness+in+America+2021_02_08_FINAL.pdf. The report goes on to complicate that definition.

34. Vivek H. Murphy, "Surgeon General: We Have Become a Lonely Nation. It's Time to Fix That," *New York Times*, https://www.nytimes.com/2023/04/30/opinion/loneliness-epidemic-america.html.

35. U.S. Department of Health and Human Services, "Our Epidemic of Loneliness and Isolation," May 3, 2023, https://www.hhs.gov/sites/default/files/surgeon-general-social-connection-advisory.pdf.

36. Although one must take care not to romanticize the past. During the 1920s, the Ku Klux Klan counted more members than at any point in American history, including after the Civil War. Few would mourn the death of that fraternity.

37. Stephanie Cacioppo, "If Loneliness Is an Epidemic, How Do We Treat It?." *New York Times*, July 14, 2023, https://www.nytimes.com/2023/07/14/opinion/treating-loneliness.html.

38. Fitzgerald, *Great Gatsby*, 35.

4. "We're All White Here"

1. F. Scott Fitzgerald, *The Great Gatsby* (1925; New York: W. W. Norton, 2022), 46.

2. "God damn the continent of Europe," Fitzgerald wrote Edmund Wilson in 1921. "It is of merely antiquarian interest.... The negroid streak creeps northward to defile the Nordic race. Already the Italians have souls of blackamoors. Raise the bars of immigration and permit only Scandinavians, Teutons, Anglo-Saxons and Celts to enter." Note the language of "creeps," which echoes the language of gradual but inevitable movement in *The Rising Tide of Color*. However, Fitzgerald recognized his nativism for what it was. In the same letter, he writes: "My reactions were all philistine, anti-socialist, provincial and racially snobbish." But then he qualified his qualification: "I believe at last in the white-man's burden."

See Andrew Turnbull, ed., *The Letters of F. Scott Fitzgerald* (New York: Scribner's, 1963), 326.

3. One possible rejoinder to this argument is that Fitzgerald based Wolfsheim on Arnold Rothstein, the Jewish businessman, gambler, and crime boss. In which case, the more egregious anti-Semitic passages in the novel, including the wolf comparison and the cufflinks made of human molars, are there to establish, quickly, the violence that Rothstein-qua-Wolfsheim is capable of. In a novel about the corruption of the American dream, it matters that Rothstein-qua-Wolfsheim also had a leading role in fixing the 1919 World Series.

4. Fitzgerald, *Great Gatsby*, 13.

5. Henry Goddard, *The Kallikak Family: A Study in the Heredity of Feeble-Mindedness* (New York: Macmillan, 1912).

6. Lothrop Stoddard, *The Rising Tide of Color* (New York: Scribner's, 1920), 162. "All three are good stocks," Stoddard observes, "ranking in genetic worth well above the various colored races. However, there seems to be no question that the Nordic is far and away the most valuable type."

7. Here Stoddard quotes Madison Grant, another eugenicist, from his 1916 book *The Passing of the Great Race*.

8. Lothrop Stoddard, *Racial Realities in Europe* (New York: Scribner's, 1924), 19.

9. Stoddard quotes an Australian professor who observed: "No one in California or Australia, where the effects of Chinese competition have been studied, has . . . the smallest doubt that Chinese laborers, if allowed to come in freely, could starve all the white men in either country out of it, or force them to submit to harder work and a much lower standard of wages" (272). The Johnson-Reed Act left untouched the 1892 Chinese Exclusion Act, which forbade any immigration whatsoever from Asian countries.

10. In a 1920 edition of *The Saturday Evening Post*, Kenneth L. Roberts published a lengthy article titled "The Rising Irish Tide," which echoes, in title and content, *The Rising Tide of Color*.

11. Later in the novel, in one of my favorite lines of the book, Tom will observe that he "'read somewhere that the sun's getting hotter every year. It seems that pretty soon the earth's going to fall into the sun—or wait a minute—it's just the opposite—the sun's getting colder every year'" (77).

12. Fitzgerald, *Great Gatsby*, 47. The problem with this passage is not the

reference to African Americans as "negroes." Until well into the twentieth century, that was the respectful way to refer to African Americans and the way African Americans referred to themselves. Few today remember that the original title of Martin Luther King's "Letter from a Birmingham Jail" was "The Negro Is Your Brother."

13. Fitzgerald, *Great Gatsby*, 35.

14. Barbara Will, "The Great Gatsby and the Unseen Word," *College English* 32/4 (2005): 137.

15. There is an irony here, too, in that coming from Chicago, Tom is himself new money. Or newer, anyway.

16. Fitzgerald, *Great Gatsby*, 85.

17. Betsy Nies has observed that Nick escapes the multicultural East for "the white, snow covered, racially unchanged Mid-West of the past." See Betsy L. Nies, *Eugenic Fantasies: Racial Ideology in the Literature and Popular Culture of the 1920s* (New York: Routledge, 2002), 95. Today who can think of Minneapolis-St. Paul without thinking of George Floyd?

18. "European Union Government Spending to GDP," *Trading Economics*, https://tradingeconomics.com/european-union/government-spending-to-gdp#:~:text=Government%20Spending%20to%20GDP%20in-,percent%20of%20GDP%20in%202007. The U.S. figure includes state spending.

19. Alberto Alesino, Edward Glaeser, and Bruce Sacerdote, "Why Doesn't the United States Have a European Welfare State?," National Bureau of Economic Research, October 2001, https://www.nber.org/papers/w8524. "Americans," the authors write, "think of the poor as members of some different group while Europeans think of the poor as members of their own group" (29).

20. Ibid., 61.

21. Paul Krugman, "Twilight of the Apparatchiks," *New York Times*, February 26, 2016, https://www.nytimes.com/2016/02/26/opinion/twilight-of-the-apparatchiks.html.

Conclusion: Our Orgastic Futures

1. F. Scott Fitzgerald, *The Great Gatsby* (1925; New York: W. W. Norton, 2022), 117. Curiously, these concluding lines of the book originally appeared as the closing lines of the first chapter, after Nick has had dinner with the Buchanans and returns to his shack, where he first sees Gatsby.

2. "Average size of floor area in new single-family houses built for sale in the United States from 1975 to 2022," Statista, https://wwwstatista.com/statistics/529371/floor-area-size-new-single-family-homes-usa/#:~:text-t=In%202022%2C%20the%20average%20size,have%20almost%20doubled%20in%20size.

3. "Average number of people per household in the United States from 1960 to 2022," Statista, https://www.statista.com/statistics/183648/average-size-of-households-in-the-us/.

4. Robert Frank, *Luxury Fever: Why Money Fails to Satisfy in an Era of Excess* (New York: Free Press, 1999), 11.

5. Adam Smith, *The Wealth of Nations* (New York: Penguin Classics, 2000), 465.

6. Gallup, "Americans Say Families Need $85,000 to Get By," https://news.gallup.com/poll/506405/americans-say-families-need-000.aspx.

7. Federal Reserve Bank of New York, "Household Debt and Credit Report," https://www.newyorkfed.org/microeconomics/hhdc. Some of that increase owes to student loans, but by no means all of it, and even choosing which college to attend is subject to comparison.

8. Frank, *Luxury Fever*, 3.

9. Pierre Bourdieu, "Haute Couture and Haute Culture," in *Sociology in Question* (London: Sage Publications, 1993), 135.

10. Frank, *Luxury Fever*, 145.

11. Ibid., 151.

12. There is such a thing as the paradox of thrift, wherein too much savings can harm an economy because consumers do not spend as much and therefore businesses have no incentive to borrow saved money to expand production. But Americans save less than their counterparts in other countries. In 2022, the country saved 1.5 percent of its GDP, sixth lowest among OECD countries. Compare Denmark, which in 2022 saved 21 percent of its GDP. America has a long way to go before thriftiness becomes an issue. OECD Data, "Saving rate," https://data.oecd.org/natincome/saving-rate.htm.

13. True, many of the forms inconspicuous consumption can take, like a shorter workday, have to happen at a social rather than an individual level. But other forms, like retiring early by spending less, can happen individually. None of this, I should add, will do much of anything for

those who live near or below the poverty level—unless, that is, we trade a desire to consume for a desire for justice.

14. Fitzgerald, *Great Gatsby*, 96.